JAMES IRVINE

JAMES IRVINE

EDITED BY
FRANCESCA PICCHI
WITH
MARIALAURA ROSSIELLO IRVINE

DEYAN SUDJIC

A VOICE
OF HIS OWN

James Irvine at three months old with his mother Betty Middleton-Sandford, a textile designer and illustrator of children's books, 1958

As a child, aged eight, 1966

James Irvine once suggested to an interviewer that his original career plan had been to become an entomologist. He said that he had changed his mind once he bought his first motorcycle, took it to pieces and found he could put it back together again. He knew immediately then, that he wanted to be a designer.

It's the kind of story that designers like to tell. They need something memorable to say to build their profile. Philippe Starck used to talk about giving café chairs three legs, so that waiters had one less thing to trip over. Sony had several different versions of the birth of the Walkman, all of which involved differing senior executives and the multiple insights of their various wives and children.

James was always an engaging storyteller, but he rooted his stories in his personal experiences, not self-promotion. Motorcycles were certainly important to him, particularly vintage thoroughbreds. He was the kind of man who was fascinated by mechanisms and how things worked. British designers have a history of finding their way into design through that kind of tinkering. Terence Conran, for example, made himself a lathe when he was at school with bits of scrap agricultural machinery.

Despite his early interest in entomology there was always a strong chance that Irvine was going to become a designer, and equally that he was going to end up working in Italy. His father, Alan, is a distinguished designer himself. He created some of the exquisite cultural exhibitions that Olivetti supported in its great days. When the horses from San Marco came to the Royal Academy in London, it was Irvine's father who devised the installation. The memorable display at New York's Metropolitan Museum of Cimabue's giant crucifix from Santa Croce in Florence after its restoration from flood damage was also his work. Alan Irvine briefly worked in Milan himself, in the studio of BBPR, and became close to Carlo Scarpa. But unlike his son, he returned to Britain.

James Irvine was sent to Frensham Heights School by his parents. It was a progressive co-educational boarding school in Surrey that encouraged creativity and self-expression – Nick Mason of Pink Floyd is among its alumni. Afterwards, Irvine studied design at Kingston Polytechnic – now Kingston University, and once Kingston School of Art and Design, in suburban southwest London. It was a school with a strong reputation in design, architecture and fashion. Irvine began his studies there in 1977, at the moment that the punk wave was breaking. It was the year that the Sex Pistols released the *Never Mind the Bollocks* album, with its cover design by Jamie Reid. The course was based on making skills, with workshops staffed by technicians to give designers an insight into manufacturing techniques.

Irvine did well enough to secure a place at the Royal College of Art, where his father had studied thirty years before. It was the only all-graduate art school in the world. When so few design students pursued masters degrees, students at the RCA stood out as the most committed and gifted of their generation. When Irvine arrived in 1981 there was still a distinction between furniture design and product design (as industrial design had just been renamed). Post-modernism was inflecting the intellectual atmosphere. But this was also a period during which a younger generation was making its mark in less predictable directions: Ben Kelly

In one of his earliest constructions – a robot he made, aged seven, 1965

As a student at the RCA, 1981

designed The Haçienda club in Manchester, Neville Brody was designing *The Face*, and Peter Saville created his cover design for New Order's *Power Corruption and Lies* album.

The Dutch furniture designer Floris van den Broecke was the senior tutor at the RCA who taught Irvine. Other students included Ross Lovegrove, Gerry Taylor (who like Irvine would move to Milan for a while), Jasper Morrison, and Daniel Weil who graduated in 1981, when he showed the Bag Radio that gave him worldwide visibility. This was the same year that Ettore Sottsass orchestrated the first Memphis collection in Milan.

Irvine's generation at the RCA was fascinated by the explosion of attention that Memphis attracted, but they were of an age to question the post-modern sensibility that had turned architecture inside out, and was spilling over into industrial design. Post-punk Britain had to come to terms with economic austerity, with industrial unrest, job losses and economic decline. Pastels, historical revivals and playfulness seemed out of place in that context.

Many of the RCA's graduates did not expect to work in the mainstream world of design, and in any case there seemed to be very few opportunities with conventional industry in the UK. The options were to operate on the edges of traditional definitions of design – in the manner of Ron Arad who had opened his One Off studio and had begun to make objects himself that ranged from pragmatic pieces of furniture assembled from industrial components, to work that verged on sculpture – or to leave the country.

Irvine's friend and fellow student Jasper Morrison explored the possibilities of putting found technologies to work in different ways. He made furniture out of laundry-basket components and bicycle handlebars. As Morrison wrote at the time, 'a furniture designer has to build his own factory, not with bricks but from the sprawling back streets teeming with sources and processes'. It was an attitude that Irvine, with his interest in materials and mechanisms, was ready to share. But rather than set up on his own in a workshop in London, he took the other option, and in 1984 left Britain to work for Olivetti in Milan. Morrison went to Berlin at about the same time.

The Olivetti design studio on the Corso Venezia, shared by one team led by Ettore Sottsass and another by Mario Bellini, had been reorganized by this time. Sottsass's leadership role had passed to Michele De Lucchi, for whom Irvine worked at first. Olivetti on the outside still looked like the world's most successful design-led company. The studio was full of talented designers from around the world. There were successful advanced technology products – the M24 PC, for example, was launched the year that Irvine arrived in Milan. And for a while it kept the company in a game that was changing rapidly, and in which the balance of power was shifting away from Europe and America, and from hardware to software. But in reality, Olivetti was finding the climate increasingly difficult. A company that had been launched by mechanical engineers had difficulty adjusting to the digital era. It could not compete with IBM, which was in trouble itself; still less with Microsoft.

Irvine worked for a year in Tokyo on an exchange programme with Toshiba's design studio. It was the time of the bubble economy, when

The designers involved in the Alessi Twergi project, 1989 (L-R: Mike Ryan, Adalberto Pironi, James Irvine, Marco Zanini, Aldo Cibic, Ettore Sottsass, Massimo Iosa Ghini)

Japan was wealthy enough to ship untested European architects such as Zaha Hadid and Philippe Starck over to build flamboyant landmarks. Irvine went back to Olivetti – then in its last years as an independent entity before vanishing into the arms of a somewhat murky reverse take over – and stayed until 1992. De Lucchi had taken up the role that Sottsass once had in maintaining Olivetti's position as a leader in design culture. But De Lucchi had no Roberto Olivetti to back him up with the management hierarchy, as Sottsass and Bellini once had.

In the meantime Irvine had met Sottsass and had started to work on his own projects. Sottsass invited Irvine to contribute to the 'Twelve New' Memphis collection in 1986. This was almost the final act of the Memphis project, but the greatest hits from the first few Memphis collections were still commercially available as part of its back catalogue. The presentation that Irvine took part in at the time of the 1986 Salone del Mobile was a project curated by Barbara Radice. The pieces were made for the most part by designers who were close to, or actually working for, Sottsass: James Irvine and Nick Bewick, along with Massimo Iosa Ghini, rather than by members of the original group. The catalogue looked a lot less convinced about the commercial appeal of what it was offering than previous editions. There were no distributors, and curiously, unlike the earlier Memphis collections, there were no names for the pieces either.

Sottsass subsequently offered Irvine a partnership at Sottsass Associati, for a while the most successful independent design studio in Italy with as many as fifty staff. Established by Sottsass with Marco Zanini at the time Sottsass left Olivetti, and riding on the extraordinary publicity generated by the Memphis movement, Sottsass Associati had clients around the world. It worked on everything from shop interiors for Esprit, to cutlery, furniture and consumer electronics such as the Enorme telephone. It also designed exhibitions and architecture. Irvine was torn between his loyalty to De Lucchi and to what Olivetti had once been, and the chance of a fresh start with Sottsass and all the opportunities that offered. After considerable soul-searching, he had made up his mind to refuse.

'I was tempted, but it meant leaving Olivetti,' he said. 'I was still faithful to Michele, who was trying to save Olivetti; driving to and from Ivrea, negotiating projects, dealing with horrible politics. Olivetti was a limping dinosaur, which Epson, Canon, and the rest were tearing to shreds. I thought about it, and decided to say no. I wrote a long letter to Ettore to explain why. I went to the studio in the Via Borgonuovo, with my letter. "Is Ettore here?" I asked. "No he is in LA. Just leave it on his desk", his secretary told me. He had a big wall at the back of his desk – two walls in fact. There were always extraordinary things pinned up. Things that he liked – there were lots of references and photographs of objects he found interesting. Ettore's table was always beautiful. There were two sets of coloured pencils, not mixed or random. A flower in a vase by Shiro Kuramata, a Japanese high-tech pen, a sheet of paper with a drawing of a stadium in Osaka he was working on, and a barometer. I picked up the letter again, and decided to become a partner.'

Irvine was in partnership with Sottsass until 1997, but ran his own studio in parallel. He worked with Sottsass, De Lucchi and Andrea Branzi on the Citizen Office project for Vitra, which explored the nature of the contemporary workplace. He also helped Sottsass on architectural projects, including the interiors at Malpensa. Irvine remembered talking with Sottsass about the airport on one of the many car journeys they took together. Malpensa's rich palette of colour and materials was, it seems, the reaction to a tour that Sottsass had recently taken through Munich's all white and silver terminal building: 'Ettore said it made him feel like a germ in a yoghurt factory.'

By that time, Irvine had already started to work for Sheridan Coakley's SCP, the pioneering British manufacturer that also produced designs by Konstantin Grcic and by Jasper Morrison, and had also contributed to the wave of new work launched by Giulio Cappellini.

This was a period when Italy's leadership in the design of furniture and consumer electronics was coming under question. After two decades of unchallenged domination, there appeared to be a shortage of Italian designers ready to succeed the *maestri*, the generation of Sottsass, Achille Castiglioni and Vico Magistretti that had led the post-World War II explosion of interest in Italian design, and had helped fuel Italy's economic boom of the 1950s and 1960s. The fact that Irvine and others like him were still ready to make their careers in Milan showed the continuing appeal of the city to the gifted, and Milan's readiness to make use of their talent.

I had seen James's work when I was still in London, but it was only once I moved to Milan to edit *Domus* magazine that we really got to know each other. He was a great guide to Milan's hinterland for a newcomer. But he was an even better critic of what was happening to design. We would talk about new work, about Italy, about technology and style. And as we got closer, we worked together. At *Domus* we commissioned him twice — once to design an exhibition on the work of Shiro Kuramata, which he did with consummate style, and a second time to create an exhibition on the *Domus* photography archive. When I left the magazine, James organized a spectacular farewell cocktail party at the infamous Bar Basso.

DEYAN SUDJIC

'The View from *Domus*' exhibition design by Irvine, 2002

Drinks token for Deyan Sudjic's *Domus* leaving party, designed by Irvine, 2004

National characteristics in design tend to lapse into cartoon-like stereotypes much too easily. To suggest that the Germans are rational, that the Japanese are interested in Zen and that the Spanish are emotional does not get anybody very far. But it is fascinating nevertheless to speculate about the nature of the very particular relationship between design as it is practised in Italy and as it is in Britain. There is a mutual attraction between the two that encompasses the British obsession with holidays in Tuscany, which is matched only by the interest of a certain class of Italians in spending their summers in West London.

It is enlightening, for example, to try to understand what it was about designers from England that persuaded Sottsass to hire so many of them to work for him. There were Charles and Jane Dillon at the time of the Synthesis furniture range; Perry King arrived at Olivetti in time for the Valentine typewriter; and a little later George Sowden was important for Olivetti as the company entered into the era of desktop computing. He was followed by Gerry Taylor and James Irvine. Chris Redfern was the last in the series of UK-born designers to work with Sottsass.

What Irvine brought with him were the practical skills that are the product of the pragmatic English way of doing things. But he also had an eye for the understated stylishness of a well-cut suit and an elegantly resolved mechanism. These are in some ways very traditional ideas of what design can be. But Irvine was always curious about new ways of doing things and new ways of making them.

Irvine had become a part of the Milanese world, and inevitably he came to synthesize the values of both the cultures in which he was rooted. He lived in Italy for thirty years. He established his studio in a nineteenth-century courtyard building close to the Navigli. He was part of the conversations at Sottsass's table in the Torre de Pisa. He was fascinated by Castiglioni and Enzo Mari, by Branzi and the Italian greats. Unlike many designers inspired from a distance by Milan's golden age, Irvine became a part of it. He took a more pragmatic view than some of the ideologically motivated Italians and would quote Magistretti's suggestion that unless you could describe a design in a few words over the telephone, it wasn't ready yet.

Irvine once described his own design process in a different way. For him the first step was to think: 'It's a mental picture then I sketch it, and give the sketch to my assistants and they draw it. I usually wait until they're finished. I'm not on their backs while they do it – it is interesting how they interpret a sketch. I don't like too much technical drawing. My job is to communicate the basic feel of something. The proportions are based on logical reasons but fundamentally I think that a project has to have a good strong idea behind it. It doesn't need to be embellished so much – it just needs to be right.'

There is more than simply designing to making a city a real centre for design in the cultural sense. Irvine made a substantial contribution to the many companies that he worked for. But he was also a key figure in the life of design in Milan in other ways. He was always ready to talk and to listen, and had the gift of inspiring the kind of conviviality on which building a community depends. Design culture is based on a continuing conversation: when the conversation stops, the culture atrophies. Irvine was an unmatched conversation starter. He could talk about football with Marc Newson, or Marxism with Mari. He was the connection between the flying circus of visiting designers from around the world and Milan itself.

It is not a stereotype to see the quintessential Englishness of Irvine in his life and work. He belonged to that remarkable generation of designers who between them have transformed the shape of design over the last two decades. After the poetry and the whimsy and the operatic excess of the 1980s, Irvine and his friends Jasper Morrison and Konstantin Grcic represented a spirit of simplicity, of plain speaking, neither austerely puritanical, nor unnecessarily blunt. Irvine made his way without flights of overblown rhetoric, without ideological overexcitement, and without the relentless self-publicity that cast a long shadow over the 1990s.

To become the embodiment of simplicity is perhaps an unexpected outcome for a close collaborator of Sottsass in the immediate aftermath of the Memphis explosion. For Irvine it was not a question of strategy or fashion: it was a reflection of his own values. Irvine admired Sottsass profoundly, but as he once told me the worst thing to do if you worked with a designer as creatively powerful as Sottsass was to try too hard to be like him. Do that, and you were lost. To survive and flourish creatively, you had to find your own voice, and be yourself. Irvine was always himself.

In his own studio Irvine was able to work at every scale. He designed the fleet of buses that Mercedes-Benz built for the city of Hanover, toys for Muji, furniture for B&B Italia, lights for Zumtobel, pens for A.G. Spalding & Bros. and then there were the exhibitions he designed for *Domus*. His work was based on exploring how to make ideas work. He had the ability to give an object clarity and charisma. He was able to work with humble materials – plywood and bent metal tubing – as well as with flawless marble.

In my living room in London I have the Lunar sofa that James designed for B&B in 1998. It brightens the room a little. But it is the tiny ink drawing that he drew for me on the back of a *Domus* business card that I treasure most. It's a diagram that reminds me how to turn that sofa into a bed, simply by putting my foot at the right point and pulling out the base. I value it, because it makes me remember the way that James's mind worked.

Portrait taken at Thonet, Frankenberg, late 1990s

DEYAN SUDJIC

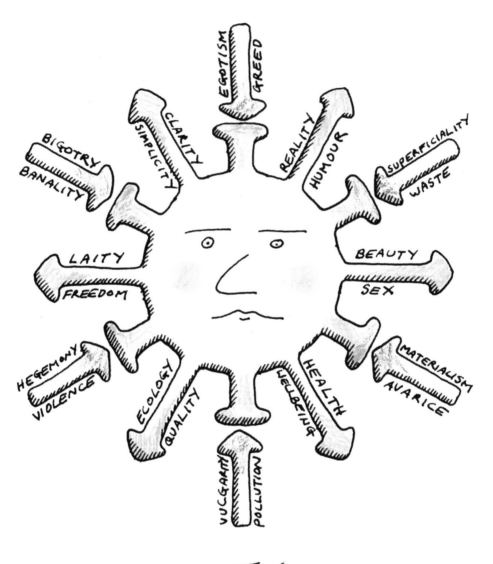

UTOPIAN
DESIGN
ANTIBODY

MARCH 2008.

JASPER MORRISON

TALKING ABOUT DESIGN AND OTHER MATTERS OF EVEN GREATER IMPORTANCE TO YOUNG MEN

Irvine with his first Triumph motorcycle, early 1980s

Irvine's chair for his RCA thesis project, 1985

In 1962 (or 1963) my family moved from a very small house in a corner of London called the World's End to a bigger house in Chelsea, where the Swinging Sixties were about to start swinging. I didn't know it then, but James Irvine was living in a studio at the end of the road. I was three and he was four, and we would soon be going to the same local school. I didn't know him there either, but our paths crossed again sixteen years later: I was on the way to my first day at Kingston Polytechnic to study design and I pulled up at some traffic lights on my Honda 90 next to a small chap on a large motorcycle. Later, I saw him park his bike in the college car park and noticed it was an old Triumph. It turned out that James was a year ahead of me on the 3D design course.

We didn't get to know each other until some three years later when I joined him at the Royal College of Art, where the students of all years shared one big studio. There was an awareness amongst us of who were the more skilled designers, even though we were not yet designers, and James was one of a few who you sensed were serious about the job. He had a cheerful confidence about him, and a way of using the drawing board that suggested he knew what he was doing. In the workshops you'd come across him bending a piece of steel tube or sawing up bits of plywood in a purposeful way, putting prototypes together with more than usual precision. I remember very well the chair that he was working on, which was an ultralight, tensioned tube frame with canvas seat and back, something like the camp beds that become tensioned by the wire legs that you spring into the poles that hold the canvas apart. It was an impressive design, absolutely fresh for the time, and with considerable skill in its structural engineering. Far more advanced than the average RCA effort.

I don't remember the exact timing, but soon after he graduated in 1985 I met him in one of the Italian cafés we used to go to and he told me he was moving to Milan to start working for Olivetti. That was like hearing from a trainee pilot that he had been selected to fly Concorde. Milan was then (as it still is, but more so) the epicentre of the design world, and to get a job in any of its design studios was almost unimaginable. I'd tried it myself a few years earlier but realized that I was more or less unemployable after the polite interest shown by the studios of Ettore Sottsass, George Sowden and Andrea Branzi to my less than professional portfolio. Simon Morgan, a friend of James's from Kingston, was at Olivetti too, working under Sowden, while James himself worked for Sottsass. I'd be in Milan once a year for the Salone del Mobile, and would stay at James's apartment on Via Torino. It was up an outdoor staircase at the back of the building, with a maximum of two windows, one at each end of a long narrow space divided in two across the middle, with rough terracotta floors and an old kitchen sink and a shower in the corner by the door. Forget about emails and faxes – there wasn't a telephone either. If you needed to call anyone (which you didn't, because you hardly knew anyone) you'd have to go to the Grand Hotel and use one of the wooden telephone boxes in the lobby, or gather enough *gettoni* to use the public one.

We'd meet up after he finished at the office and look for a cheap trattoria for dinner, always accompanied by a few bottles of wine. After that, we'd continue the evening looking for one of the late-night kiosks

One of Irvine's many sketches

On the steps of the Royal Albert Hall, London, 1980s

that served drinks through the night – either the two of us, or with Simon and their ever-increasing group of friends like Nick Bewick, Matt Sindall and George Sowden. Occasionally, it was almost morning by the time we found our way home, still talking about design and other matters of even greater importance to young men. Once, we came back with the theory that milk was the ideal substance and continued the theme for another hour at Via Torino, forgetting that there was the visiting editor of an English design magazine sleeping under the dining table.

The incredible thing about James, was that he could get up two hours later and go to work, as if, apart from slightly red eyes, he'd had an early night, while I'd sleep on until noon and wake up with a hangover. On the night of the milk episode he had to get up particularly early for a television interview about the Sottsass studio – I don't know how he did it. He was very professional, and even though I began to have some success with a few designs in production, I always looked up to his professionalism, realizing that I didn't have it.

I had been designing for Cappellini for a few years when James and I had the idea of proposing a collection of smaller accessories to Giulio Cappellini. It was called Progetto Oggetto (Object Project) and, as strange as it sounds, it was a new idea at the time. Furniture companies made furniture then and didn't think about making other things. We assembled a long list of participants from the group of designers we knew in England, Italy and Sweden, and we designed the exhibition that was held in Cappellini's Brianza headquarters – an old house with a workshop and a small warehouse attached to it. It was a critical success, but the pieces (more or less handmade by Brianza craftsmen) were too expensive for the shops. We used to drive up to meet Giulio Cappellini, leaving Milan

Jasper Morrison and Irvine, early 1980s

Irvine and Morrison playing pétanque, 2006

early in the morning, stopping off for a coffee at Bar Basso on the way. One of those days a very smart businessman or lawyer walked in, ordered a dry martini, drank it in one go, paid and walked out in the space of a minute. We raised our eyebrows over our cappuccinos and the barman raised his back at us. It was a very Milanese moment and the kind of thing James loved about Italy. As English as James was, he was perfectly matched by the old Milanese spirit of doing things with a certain panache. He would always get along best with the engineers he worked with in the factories, or his barber; he was much loved by the restaurant trade too, and not just for the business he brought them! Whenever I get the chance, I go for lunch or dinner at Torre di Pisa, the Tuscan trattoria famous among the Milanese designer set, and the boss never fails to shake his head and say 'Nostro vecchio amico, eh?'

When selecting a restaurant for as many people who were in town and up for it, James would take out a couple of sheets of folded A4 paper with a list of hundreds of restaurants in micro type, scan through it quickly, checking for a 'closed on Tuesdays' note or another game-changer, before selecting the appropriate spot. Booking restaurants for friends was almost a second career. The list typified his attention to detail, while his gregarious nature and pleasure in life were perfectly suited to his role as chief epicurean coordinator of designers who happened to be in Milan on any given evening. There is a network of designers that certainly wouldn't have existed without those A4 lists, or the person who compiled them, and many who owe James for easing their way into the Milan system.

He used to tell great stories, always hilarious and usually of a self-denigrating nature. A classic example concerned a stay he had at the Hotel España in Barcelona, a modernist palace by Gaudí's teacher Domènech i Montaner, with a large glass-covered courtyard onto which most of the rooms opened. At the time, it was one of the cheaper options available to the traveller looking for a bed, but the downside was that if any of the other guests decided to hold a party in their room, nobody would get any sleep. On the night in question, there was a Spanish group staying who were determined to play guitars and sing as loud as they could late into the night. James eventually got out of bed to close the full-length window, but the curtain was hooked over the door, so he took a chair – in an attempt to get the curtain clear of the frame he lost his balance and the chair fell over, swinging himself out of the window with no clothes on, to the great amusement of the Spanish.

It doesn't make sense to list James's many great design achievements as they are all included in this book, but I believe that his last designs were among his best – in particular the Juno chair for Arper, and the USB Desk Fan he designed for Muji. His other great skill – probably inherited from his father Alan, who is himself a great exhibition designer – was the work he did for Thonet and many others, designing stands and displays. We worked on an exhibition of Kenneth Grange's design at the Design Museum in London in 2011 and I found out how much he knew about the art of display and how to get the most effect from an exhibit. He was a great designer and an even greater friend.

Juno chair for Arper, 2012

'Kenneth Grange: Making Britain Modern' exhibition, Design Museum, London, designed by Irvine and Morrison, with Graphic Thought Facility, 2011

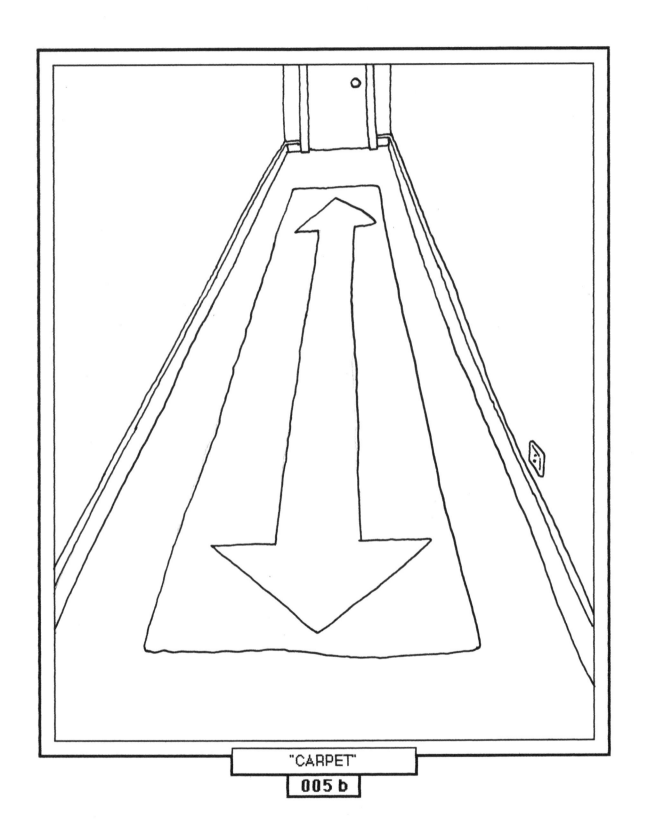

"CARPET"

005 b

FRANCESCA PICCHI

A THING
OF
BEAUTY
IS A JOY
FOREVER

Sottsass Associati, 1993 (L-R: Mike Ryan, Marco Zanini, Mario Milizia, James Irvine, Johanna Grawunder, Ettore Sottsass)

It's not easy to explain the deep relationship between James Irvine and Milan, and to understand how this 'being in tune' came about and turned into the closest of bonds. Did he ever think of returning to London? James was English through and through, but he loved Milan (and Italy) with a joyful affection. He was always amused, surprised, full of wonder. He laughed and made others laugh. A lot.

It's important to stress how hugely significant James's role of go-between was. He was a real hub, a catalyst for creative energies, a connection maker, one of those people who can weave super-dense relational webs, and are crucial yet often overshadowed by the events they themselves have made possible. The kind of person who acts as a bridge between different worlds, and while acting as a link often forgets to put him- or herself at the centre of the picture.

In this sense, the project that I feel best represents his capacity for bridging different worlds is the way he revisited for Muji a design classic like Thonet's Chair No. 14. Bringing together Thonet and Muji (respectively, an undisputed icon by one of the leading 'brands' of classic European design and the foremost Japanese company in no-brand strategy) can be seen not only as the height of diplomacy but also as one of those relational conjuring tricks that only James was able to perform successfully. The actual process of re-designing is perfectly emblematic of the idea of 'contemporary classic' so dear to James, where elements rooted in history and brought up to date coexist with something ironic and unexpected: here the chair-icon itself is camouflaged and made to disappear against the profile of the table-top.

James played this invaluable role of go-between more or less throughout his career, but it reached its apogee in the transition between the 1980s and 1990s, when he was key in taking a formal vision of design from a period of exuberance of form — when strong, unique, original and surprising gestures proclaimed the presence of their creators and their powerful subjectivity — towards a greater objectivity, which I think of as the centrality of the object. However, James loved mass production and was attracted by industry; his sights were not set on art galleries or niche objects, but directed more towards mass-market products. His solid, pragmatic training had made him certain of a number of elementary truths, and with his eye set firmly on these, he looked for allies with whom to share the same language. Foremost among them was Jasper Morrison — the two designers forged a very close association that went back to their years in London and the RCA.

During that time, James played a pivotal part in putting together a group of young designers, who made up the first globalized design generation, since it was based on personal affinity and a common language rather than on geographical origins or education. All these young designers became key players in the international design field: names such as Konstantin Grcic, Jasper Morrison, Marc Newson, Stefano Giovannoni and Thomas Sandell, and, later, Naoto Fukasawa. Designers with strong personalities, markedly different from one another, but with something in common: a shared vision that could be defined as a deep passion for the object as a phenomenon with a life of its own. That's why I see them as 'intellectuals of the object'.

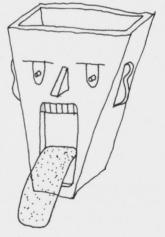

Sketch of a vase, Solid period, late 1980s

A THING OF BEAUTY IS A JOY FOREVER

Swimming pool lamp, published in Solid catalogue, 1986

The 'centrality of the object' is something that has to be carefully nurtured and cultivated, but above all it requires the participation of a vital partner: industry. The designer makes him- or herself guarantor of an outcome to which many other factors contribute: technology, production methods, personal skills, relationships, individual histories, chance... But on this journey whose destination is the object, industry helps keep the ship on course, acting as a kind of compass. Or, at least, this idea of industry as a 'reality check' is what I think I understood through my contact with James's work and his countless sketches, drawings, thoughts, prototypes, tests and the changes of direction that mark the individual steps in his gradual approach to the object – as the receptor at the centre of this dense web of relationships.

James loved diversity – he was amused by differences and curious about variations, distance and 'the other'. He took pleasure in putting together different things and diverse people, and this plurality is undeniably a post-modern trait. In this sense what he did together with Jasper Morrison for Cappellini – a coherent whole made up of different pieces by different hands – is also profoundly post-modern, despite its poetics of simplicity and anonymity. Indeed, in the 1990s, James was committed to a new simplicity which was seen as a reduction of all the unnecessary elements that obscured the basic meaning of the object. As Bruno Munari said, 'To complicate is easy, to simplify is hard.'

Educated in the tenets of modernism, James was steeped in the idea of creating elegant and timeless objects, useful forms that were fit for purpose and able to perform their function. But more than that: over the years James worked hard to widen the scope of formal references, from Britain to Italy and Japan to India, perhaps because he was convinced that objects had their own language and that a designer's sole task was to facilitate the emergence of that language.

MILAN AND ITS CULTURAL SOUP

In order to understand James's role better, it is helpful to mention something about his life. When he arrived in Milan in 1984 to work at Olivetti, he immediately had to face a change that was destined to put into question all the rules of the modern world: the transformation of our everyday landscape by electronics. This delicate moment of transition from the mechanical world to the electronic, was at the heart of the research that Ettore Sottsass, then heading Olivetti's design department, was carrying out with his group of young collaborators. In particular, Sottsass had found in George Sowden and Michele De Lucchi two close advisors; they co-authored designs for calculating machines and electronic devices that were becoming increasingly sophisticated and needed to stay abreast of technological developments. He also found in them two capable designers who could share a way of thinking that went beyond merely making objects but encompassed a vision of the new human landscape, which electronics would generate.

So James arrived in Milan in the middle of that transformation, and immediately started to work on office machines and systems for Olivetti, with De Lucchi, with whom he worked in very close contact. They worked jointly on the design of the Delphos office system and on many other

Portrait for *Vogue Uomo*, no. 390, 2008

FRANCESCA PICCHI

Sketches for vases, Solid period, 1986

projects involving electronic devices, constantly commuting between Milan and Massa Carrara (in western Tuscany), where Olivetti's furniture production was located. During the long hours spent driving back and forth across Italy, James and Michele worked, chatted, talked, joked and formed an ever closer bond. In the meantime, adapting to the kind of creative schizophrenia common among the Milan design community, alongside his job at Olivetti James began to carry out research and experimentation jointly with the group of architects and designers gravitating towards Ettore Sottsass. After Memphis burst onto the scene in 1981, Sottsass was attracting the attention of the international design community more than ever.

Memphis may have had the strength to burst onto the now globalized design scene, liberating its idiom and asserting the poetic power of objects, but it must be said that this episode, so central to contemporary design, didn't come out of the blue, all of a sudden. It had been stimulated by a very lively environment of thinking and debate generated by the Radical movements and later influenced by Pop imagery and the culture of mass consumption. In addition, Milan was where the historic core of post-war Italian design was based, comprising the so-called 'masters': Achille Castiglioni, Vico Magistretti, Angelo Mangiarotti, Enzo Mari, Bruno Munari and Marco Zanuso, highly individual voices and essential reference points for anyone associated with design. Also, on the Milan design scene of the 1980s there was a presence that paralleled and in a way rivalled that of Memphis: Alessandro Mendini's Studio Alchimia. That polarity helped create a dynamic context marked by intellectual tension and lively debate, in which every idiom was questioned, analysed, adapted and appropriated by an entire community, which, though international, gravitated around Milan and its network of factories, a manufacturing power that would soon be overshadowed by the relentless march of globalization.

So, in the mid-1980s, about to turn thirty, James found himself plunged into the middle of a Milan overflowing with creative energy and caught up in the debate between modernism and post-modernism, a rich, vibrant, positive and optimistic city, where everything seemed possible and everyone was busy. James arrived in time to participate in one of the last Memphis events, an exhibition in 1986 entitled 'Dodici Nuovi – Twelve New', while at the same time he was working with a group of young designers assembled by De Lucchi and named Solid, in acknowledgement of a rediscovered concrete quality of design, preparing the ground for the post-Memphis period. It was a time of huge experimentation and James was trying to establish his position in this world.

When Alessandro Mendini talks about the 1980s he describes a period full of energy, because at one point people from very different places came together and created a kind of cosmic force that had the power to change everything (Mendini describes in more or less those terms the strange combination of factors he called 'Milanese cultural soup' – and which was able to generate the most interesting international design phenomena of the period). James lived the spirit of 1980s Milan to the full: meetings, discussions, lunches, dinners (many dinners), not to mention the countless aperitifs, parties, private views and cocktail events. In Italy there is a term 'bar chat', meaning conversation about something

Napkins, Hong Kong project, Design Gallery
Milano, 1992

apparently banal, but which helps people get to know one another, clarify their ideas and establish their place in the world, without fakery or barriers of culture or class. In actual fact, to James, a table in a bar or restaurant was the perfect stage for a debate on design in its most vital and human aspects.

As an Englishman, and an expert in the subtle art of conversation, he knew how to turn any meeting into an opportunity for fun as well as an interesting exchange of views. He was interested in design not so much from the point of view of academic discussion, but in its most ordinary context: as something that could be part of everyone's daily life because it was straightforward and accessible, with no filters or barriers of any kind, relying on its usability to make it widely known. As Munari used to say, 'The artist's dream is to be represented in a museum, the designer's dream is to be represented in street markets.' And I believe that goal was always close to James's heart. In fact, in one of his notebooks from his years in Japan, I found a note that said, 'The industrial product is indisputably the artefact of the twentieth century. The importance of design as cultural research and how it has taken over from art as the leading method of cultural communication purely because of its ability to be instantly distributed, cannot be underestimated.'

That premise is a useful description of the kind of atmosphere that comes about in cities at particular times in their histories, when ideas are there to be absorbed with the air one breathes; thought is what gets assimilated through discussions, meetings, and all this ferment is useful in getting one's bearings, sharpening one's sight and putting visions and ideas into focus. It is not fortuitous that, in its most fertile period of its history as far as design is concerned, Milan did not have specific places or institutions devoted to design. Everything seemed to happen in an intangible way, through a community that made its own rules (as well as its manias and obsessions) and discussed them internally and more or less informally – at parties, at events, at product launches, at furniture trade shows.

When James was asked in an interview whether he ever discussed his work with colleagues, he answered candidly, 'All the time, I have friends from all over the world and every week we discuss work, politics, quality of life, food, whatever. I am interested in humanistic aspects, but you can't work with morals. I try to design things that are true to themselves and not too influenced by marketing factors, things are for people, because my clients are people, not industry.'

THE RELATIONAL INSIGHT
It could be said that James found himself at the crossroads of various moments of transition. He lived through the clash between modernism and post-modernism, the shift from mechanics to electronics, and the polarity of post-modernism and the 'new simplicity', and always first-hand. First-hand, because he was working for Olivetti, a company at the cutting edge of this technology, which was able to build the first ever calculator working entirely on transistors, and which later lost every challenge until it ran into the ground and remained stuck in a past without a future. First-hand, because he had the opportunity of knowing intimately one of the

Cover of *Modo* magazine, no. 113, 1989

FRANCESCA PICCHI

Drawing by Steven Guarnaccia explaining the movement that transforms the Gyro sofa bed for Campeggi, 1997

Sketches for Toulemonde Bouchart carpets, 1990s

leading figures of post-modernism – Ettore Sottsass – and sharing with him the spirit of the age.

James spent the whole of 1987 (when Japan was a beacon of modernity) in Tokyo, coming into contact with a culture of consumption at the height of its irresistible, unrestrainable seductive power, and allowing himself to be seduced and amused by it. He wrote, 'For me to be in Japan working at Toshiba has been like a step into the future.' He was carried away by the impact of Japanese consumer culture, while finding himself an employee of one of the leading electronic companies in the Far East, its product designer – a 'salaryman' condition that amused him as he experienced it in all its most ordinary aspects, becoming an enthusiast of the world of manga and Japanese Pop culture.

During that year he worked on the designs for three key objects related to communication: a telephone, a television set and the concept for a computer that was strikingly similar to an iPad, way ahead of its time. These designs are interesting because of their formal approach, and James took his analysis of the body of each object to its extreme – taking all the elements and reassembling them in new dynamic arrangements.

In Japan – an entirely new and extremely competitive context where design was not a niche market targeted at an elite group of consumers as it was in Europe – James felt free to combine the humanistic and anthropological approach he had acquired in Italy with the constantly changing idiomatic dynamics of continuous technological progress. When he returned to Milan he was much stronger and ready to express his own point of view. It was then that he opened his studio.

It is my opinion that at the centre of James's vision of design was his relationship with Sottsass, with whom he was in partnership from 1993 to 1999. James was so respectful of Sottsass's idiom that he knew he would not be able to replicate it. Surrounded by a proliferation of what Andrea Branzi has ironically called 'Sotts-Art', James, although justified by his status as partner, chose the route of a more pared-down formal simplicity.

But I believe that Sottsass's strongest influence on James was the anthropological dimension, the emotional resonances, the profoundly therapeutic, even magical bond that human beings establish with the objects with which they surround themselves. Sottsass also taught James that design is an interpersonal phenomenon, an activity that, though solitary, is nevertheless embedded in a web of relationships with others, from which we take vital nourishment. This relational aspect of group work, of collective discussions about design was typical of Sottsass's working attitude, inherited from the Radical research of the 1970s onwards. It was a deeply rooted aspect of his character, and a central part of James's way of doing things. From Progetto Oggetto onwards – from his work for Muji to the collections in marble for Marsotto, but also on the smaller, domestic scale of traditional Italian businesses – he always tried to approach a design project as an event to be handled collectively.

When I had the opportunity to interview him about his relationship with Sottsass, James told me how when Rolf Fehlbaum, CEO of Vitra, invited him to think about a project for the office, Sottsass replied that he would not be able to do it on his own, but that with a group of friends he would have the confidence to attempt it. That's how Branzi

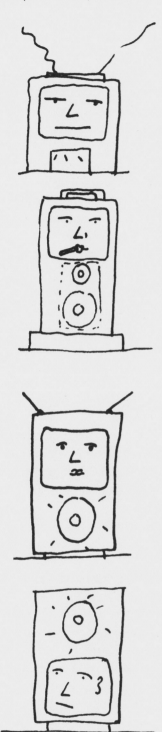

and De Lucchi became involved in what would become the Citizen Office
project, with James as coordinator, an important experience and a
turning point in James's career, since on the basis of it Sottsass asked
him to be his partner.

AN ENVIRONMENT CAPABLE OF ABSORBING, CHANGING AND AGING

Why do I think that relational aspect was so important to James? First of all
because I believe he associated the idea of research, as a vital component
of design, with the collective dimension of the work. But not only that.
The 1980s mark the apotheosis and the epilogue of what Fredric Jameson,
theorist of post-modernism and the cultural logic of post-capitalist
societies, identifies as the 'centred subject'. This disappearance of the
individual subject, together with its direct formal consequence, 'means
the end of much more — the end, for example, of style, in the sense of the
unique and the personal.' Thus I believe that, despite their fascination
with modernism, this is a factor closely connected with a post-modern,
post-capitalist, post-industrial dimension, however you wish to define
it, associated with James and his group of friends when, in the middle
of a linguistic fragmentation, they adopted the idiom of the anonymous
object. With a natural aptitude for observing, for listening to the most
disparate voices, both internal and external, and thus for recovering the
idea of design as anonymous collective thought, James was capable of
establishing an emotional, poetic relationship with objects. As he, himself
said, 'We can learn a great deal by observing the dialogue carried on
between a person and an object.'

James's transition from the late 1980s to the early 1990s was marked
by a number of small collective projects, in which he experimented with
a new freedom of expression. Many times during that period his work came
close to the world of strip cartoons and a different idea of representation
involving objects which led him towards a series of 'animistic' designs:
lamps, chairs, chandeliers or small tables that tend to assert themselves as
characters. I see this animistic allusion as a constant feature of his formal
approach, however diluted it became in time. His affinity with the world
of figurative representation expresses a 'Pop' core in his work, a force that
was very strong, but just as strongly kept under control, a way of thinking
that led him constantly to look to the world of mass consumption as a
further source of formal references.

I am convinced that the post-modern experience came to form
part of his thinking. In his search for contemporary classics, James was
inextricably linked with the idea of designing elegant, timeless objects,
intended to serve a purpose, a function of their own. The concept
of function that pervaded modernism was, however, experienced in
James's work as the centre of a much more complex, clearly articulated
relationship between human beings and the things that surround them.

Talking to people who had known him for a long time, I understood
how James had been one of the leading figures in an important period in
contemporary design, but also how he had been that in a quiet, almost
invisible way, as he was in his personal life. In fact, despite his exuberant
personality James liked to stay in the background. He was definitely
British: he didn't like to raise his voice, either in his designs or in his life.

FRANCESCA PICCHI

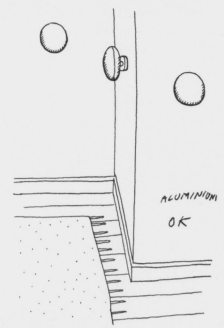

Page from the original Progetto Oggetto catalogue featuring the coat hook Irvine designed for the collection, 1992

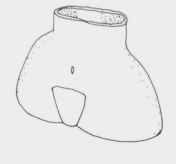

Sketches for vases, Solid period, 1986

He wasn't aggressive, audacious or disillusioned, but always friendly, always full of admiration and always ready to be surprised – enthusiastic about everything, even the seemingly most insignificant details. Although he had lived through a period dominated by the towering presence of some great designers, theoreticians and thinkers, from Sottsass to Mari, in reality James didn't seem interested in discussing the theoretical underpinnings of the society in which he found himself; he was more interested in accepting everything and welcoming it into his universe of forms, reinventing it in the joy of being a designer.

In his own way, James was a man who worked against the grain. In a Milan that was often disenchanted, bold and quite aggressive, he remained firmly grounded in his own convictions, anchored in the ethical dimension of work. As he told Franco Raggi, the social function of design in which he had been trained in Britain did not prevent his appreciating the spontaneity in design and production that has always been characteristic of Italy: 'British design culture has this component of public usefulness, almost a social ethic of design, quite different from the heady and in its own way revolutionary individualism of post-war Italy, a context with no social tradition, with none of the rigidity of an industrial culture, in which an entrepreneur could invent goods and products with new, free forms.'

PRODUCTS FOR ALL OF US TO ENJOY

James's 'sausage' period deserves special mention. In the same way painters have obsessions that mark different periods in their work, James acknowledged that one chapter in his career was dominated by a specific motif. How should it be defined? From a strictly geometrical point of view it could be seen as a development of the parallelepiped – two parallel lines connected by a semicircle. But James had the necessary ironic detachment to see it as the shape of a sausage.

The so-called 'sausage period' lasted long enough to become the symbol of a creative moment in which everyone was looking for a 'trademark' with which to establish their identity and not simply become lost in the mass of designers seeking recognition. But it is a shape that evokes an idea of rigour, mitigated by a strong aversion for the hard edges and stiffness of geometry: 'the simplest of forms, as soft and non-aggressive as possibile,' as James insisted. The sausage period had its peak in a design that was central to James's career: a city bus.

In 1999, on the cusp of the new millennium, James embarked on his design for the city of Hanover using a Mercedes-Benz O530 Citaro chassis. Given the scale of the commission (131 buses were manufactured), the prestige of the client (Hanover was about to host Expo 2000), and the reputation of the company Mercedes-Benz, with whom he was invited to work, this project made great demands on the small studio James had opened when he came back from Japan. It was, in fact, the project that gave him the confidence to leave Sottsass Associati and devote himself exclusively to his own studio.

For the bus, a project that combined social utility and design, James sought above all to create order in the overall design of the vehicle, focusing on the idea of a single volume with the greatest areas of

Irvine and Morrison, Milan, 1980s

glass that the existing chassis would permit. He then revised its internal organization, creating a large, clear central space, with the seats arranged along the edges. As soon as he had succeeded in doing that, having revived the idea of a perfect 'box', a simple container based on elementary geometric principles, he could finally add the features that make for a pleasant relationship between the user and the machine, and concentrate on the details that determine their interaction: the seats, the push-buttons, the grab-handles, the bell, the rests on which passengers lean, the fabrics and the colours. In order to emphasize the kind of sensory relationship that was so vital to the design, he insisted that the client, who was concerned about costs, incorporate leather straps, explaining how important it was to pay attention to the crucial point of contact in the relationship between the user and the mechanical device. The handle or strap is the actual point on which that relationship is focused, and James took it as symbolizing the contact between human beings and the objects with which they are surrounded.

The bus project, which was on a scale between architecture and design, contained all the features typical of James's approach to creating the character of an object, its personality, that special quality that enables it to exert a positive influence on its environment: something that arises from attention to details and the way they are put together to create a single coherent whole, neutral, clear, logical, comprehensible, like a perfectly cut piece of tailoring, a well-made garment. That's a constant feature of James's work: a formal 'dress', which springs from respect for objects, their history and tradition, and which from the totality of all those minute observations of countless everyday gestures, produces a clear sense of a whole. From that sense emerges their existence as elements – characters able to occupy space in such a way as to make the moments of life we spend together pleasant.

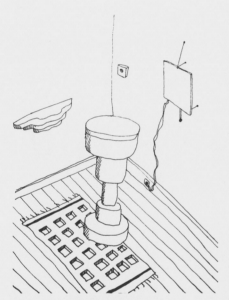

Sketch from the Solid series, 1986

In James's writing I have noticed that the word 'respect', applied to the object, occurs frequently, as if he considered the intrinsic language that objects have developed during the course of their existence something that must be respected in so far as it contains within it its own undeniable character, determined by history, by its typology or more simply by memory or use, something that exists outside its maker's creative ego, and which is otherwise liable to be smothered by the exercise of that subjectivity. In a passage that he wrote while he was in Japan, James speaks of objects and their journey to assertiveness, as a form of evolution that has taken place over time: 'Often designers change things for change's sake when the product has spent decades being gently nurtured to maturity. There is no need to destroy this functional and cultural presence. It demands great respect and yet there must be no fear of laying our hands on it and reassessing its expression.'

FRANCESCA PICCHI

PROJECTS FOR 'TWELVE NEW' MEMPHIS EXHIBITION • 1986

James took part in one of the last Memphis shows curated by Barbara Radice, at a time when the group was 'thinking about a wide range of research projects in the fields of architecture and design'. A number of comic-strip artists were also involved. The work of the twelve newcomers was shown alongside the presentation of the Design 1986 collection. James presented a console table that used aluminium, glass mosaic and wood in a series of overlapping elements. – Francesca Picchi

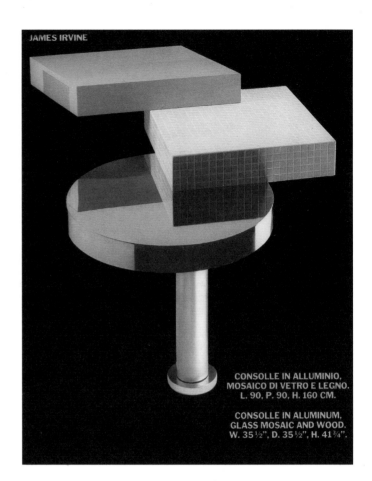

JAMES IRVINE

CONSOLLE IN ALLUMINIO, MOSAICO DI VETRO E LEGNO. L. 90, P. 90, H. 160 CM.

CONSOLLE IN ALUMINUM, GLASS MOSAIC AND WOOD. W. 35½", D. 35½", H. 41¾".

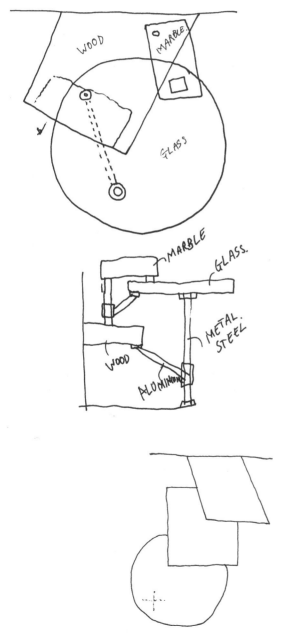

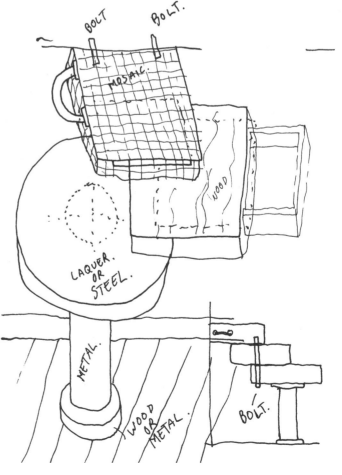

SOLID • 1986

This new phenomenon was started by eight young
designers, some Italian, some foreigners, drawn to
Milan by the energy that the city emits today. There
are many young people who are involved in Milanese
design: they arrive from far away cities and are
charged with energy and enthusiasm, ready to be put
to the test so they can start to 'make design'.
These young designers are insatiable consumers of
images, and figurative communication. They are armed
with an extraordinary determination to realize
thoughts and dreams. These particular thoughts are
very concrete, precise, substantial, geometric...
Solid. - Michele De Lucchi (excerpt from catalogue)

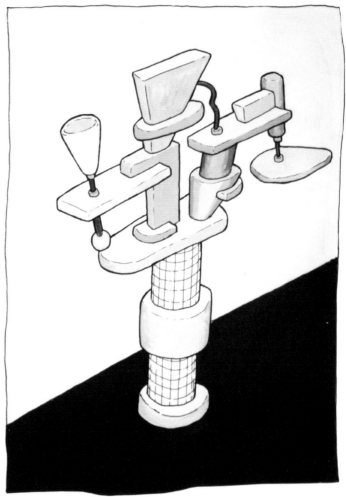

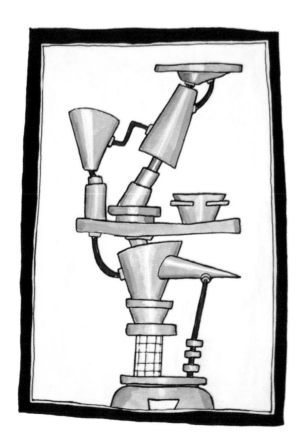

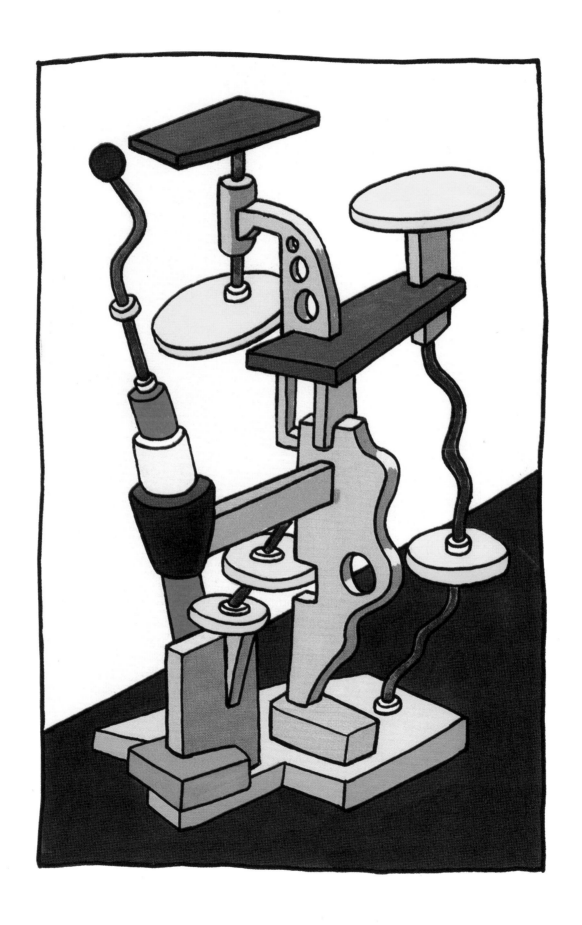

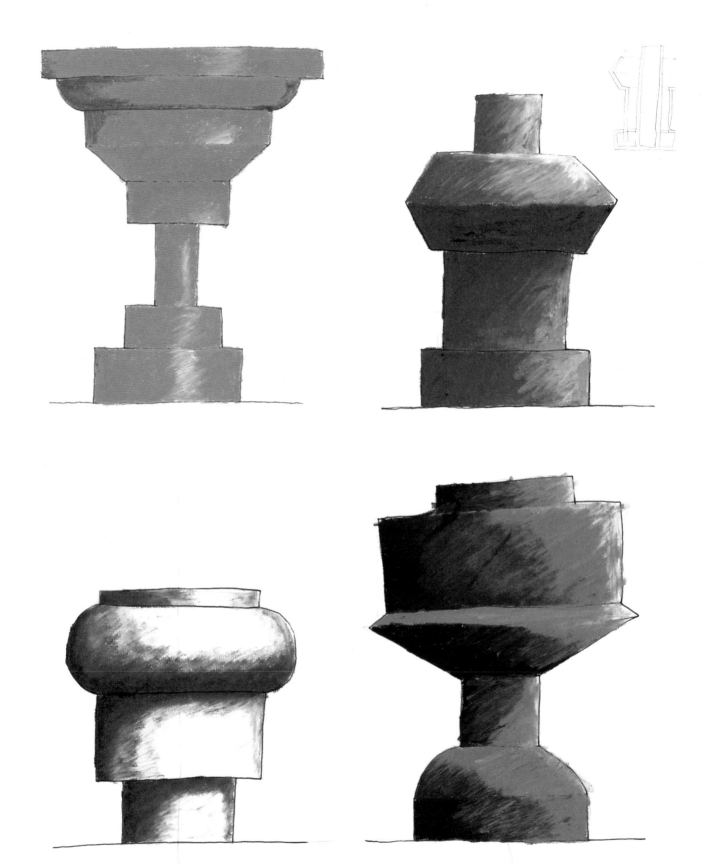

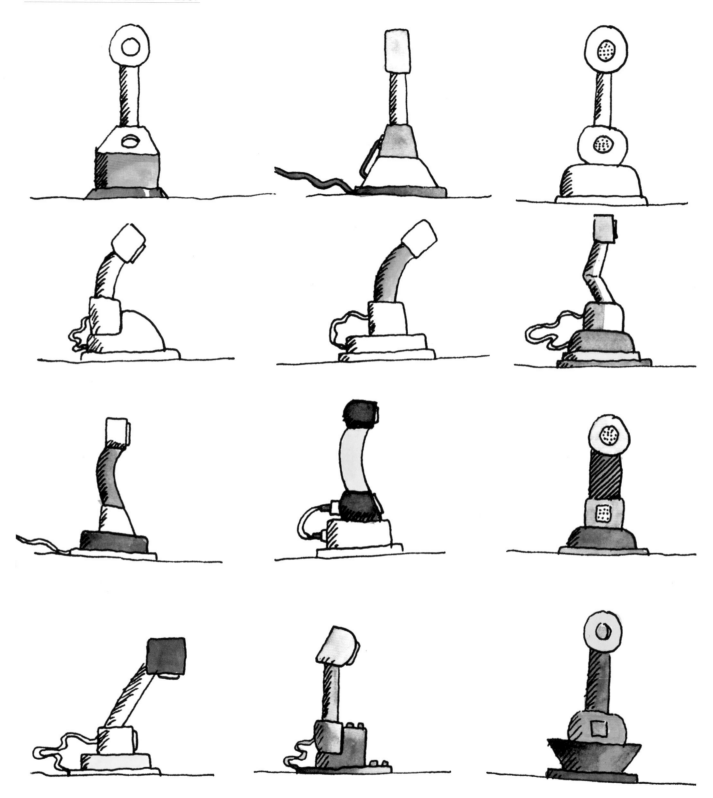

ELECTRIC SCULPTURE

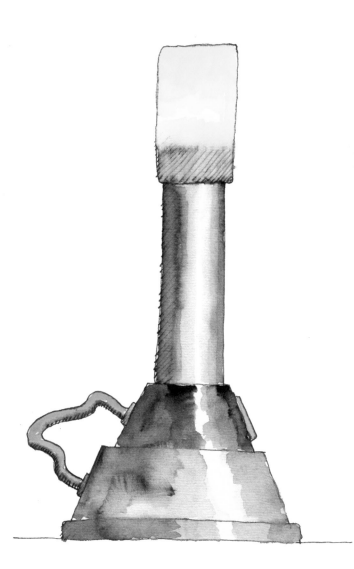

1. TELEPHONE (1987)

This telephone was conceived to give
maximum ergonomic function with minimum
footprint. It gives a renewed symbolic
quality to a common household object. This
design incorporates a new configuration
of classic components and can be produced
in a series of various symmetrical forms.
- James Irvine

2. VANITY UNITS [1987]

Project concept: design a semi-systematic domestic range of vanity units, taking into account the following factors:

- Low price - high image
- Minimum use of materials
- Simplicity of construction
- Compactness
- No decoration
- Shared components
- Good ergonomics

The key is to retain maximum flexibility through simplicity.
- James Irvine

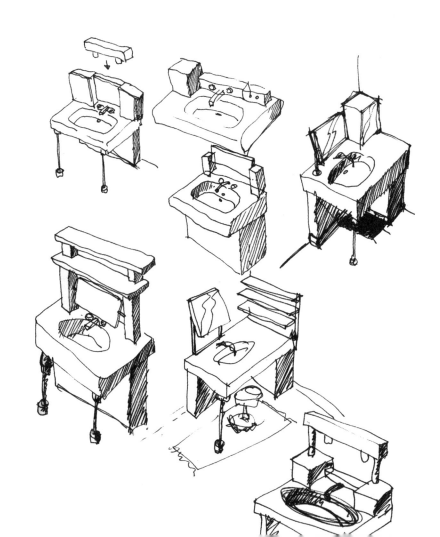

3. COMPUTER (1987)

Through a series of different components, this design offers varying levels of complexity and product character. The concept is to introduce maximum flexibility to information input. The product can be configured in various different ways, and is conceived to be static or portable, assisted by central mainframes or self-sufficient. The product has no single operative approach, therefore giving maximum ergonomic flexibility.
- James Irvine

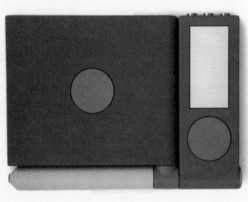

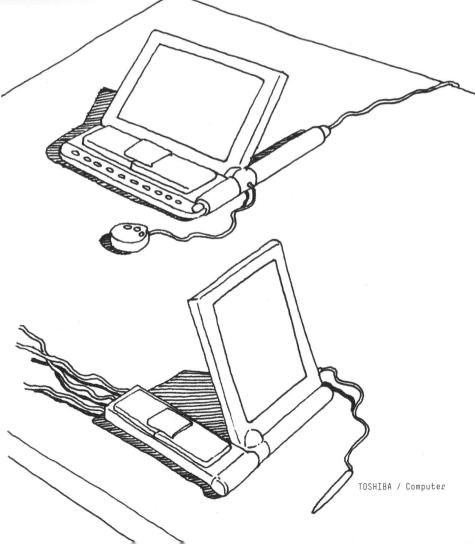

Metals is a collection of furniture designed for bars
and other meeting-places for urbanites who like to
get together in the evening for impromptu cultural
'happenings'. This is an example of 'behavioural design',
conceived for use in a shared space. The strong lines
of the table's base, consisting of two stacked cones set
opposite each other (a clear reference to Brancusi) are
the compositional elements that create its power.

- Davide Mercatali

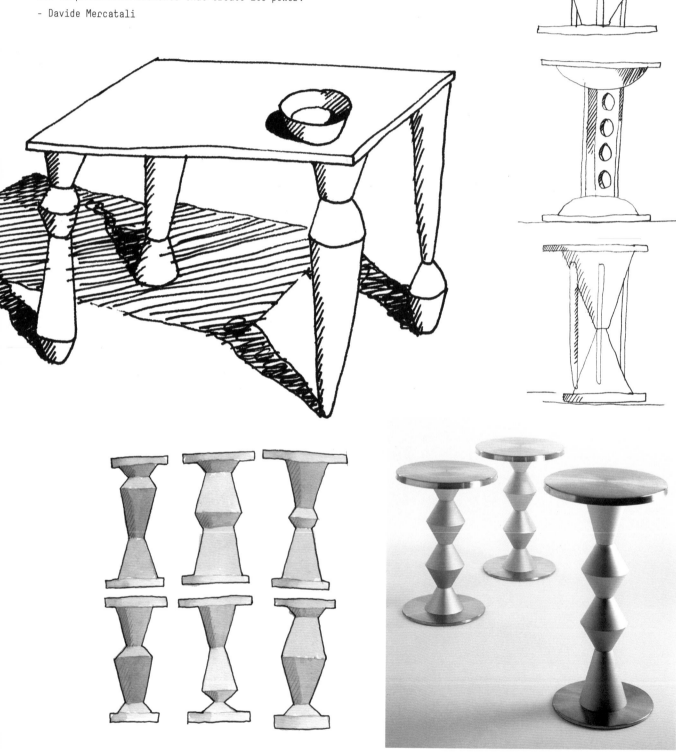

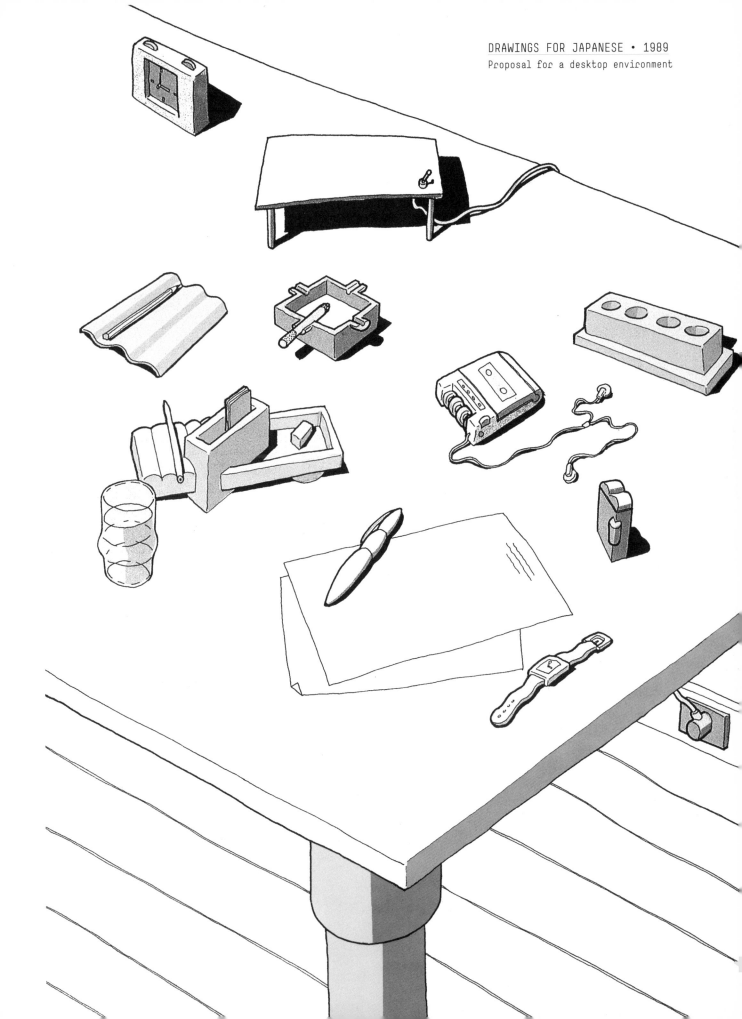

James's tap was part of an exhibition of prototypes
entitled 'Fantini Art'. Despite the freedom offered by the
brief, James's design is both professional and functional.
It is full of ironic references, taking pleasure in precise
workmanship and loaded with the formalism of the Memphis
period, whilst retaining the everyday nature of an object
such as a tap. Plus, it contains a novelty: a miniature
vase and integrated soap dish. - Davide Mercatali

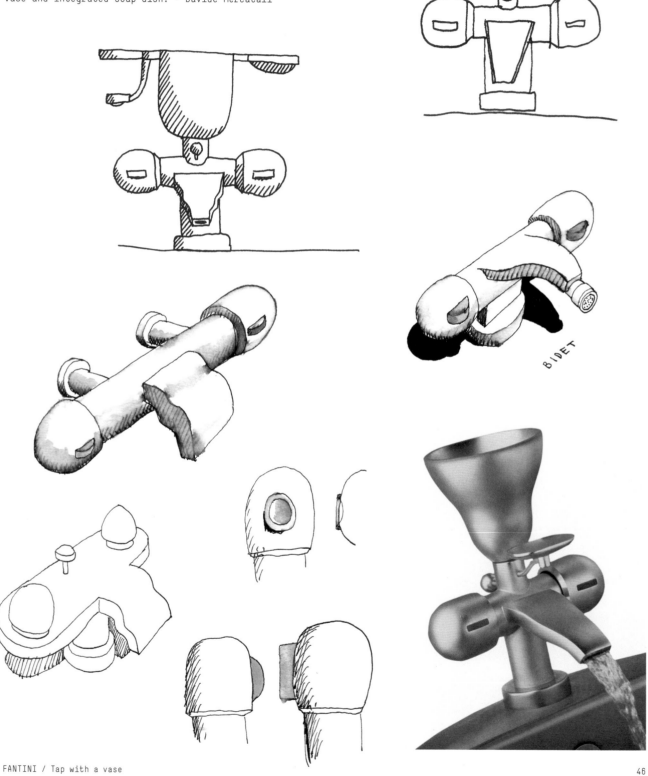

BIDET

TWERGI, ALESSI • 1989-1990

Two research projects were begun, involving two kinds of very different designers - both culturally and geographically: Ettore Sottsass and his group in Milan, and Milton Glaser in New York. Ettore Sottsass was asked to work on the theme of pepper mills, condiment sets, bowls and trays, and included the work of a few young exponents of Milanese design belonging to the same group: Massimo Iosa Ghini, James Irvine, Adalberto Pironi and Mike Ryan. A particular emphasis has been given to the quality of the different woods used, to the quality of the workmanship and the final finished quality of the objects. - Alberto Alessi (excerpt from Twergi catalogue)

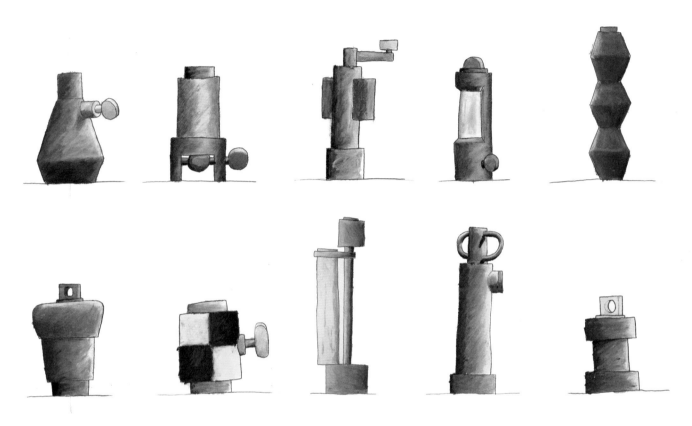

NUOVI OGGETTI RANGE, LUMOIS FIRST FOLIO • 1991

'New Objects' - the reversible Luman Candlestick and the pig-shaped Lumoid Lamp, both made from ceramic

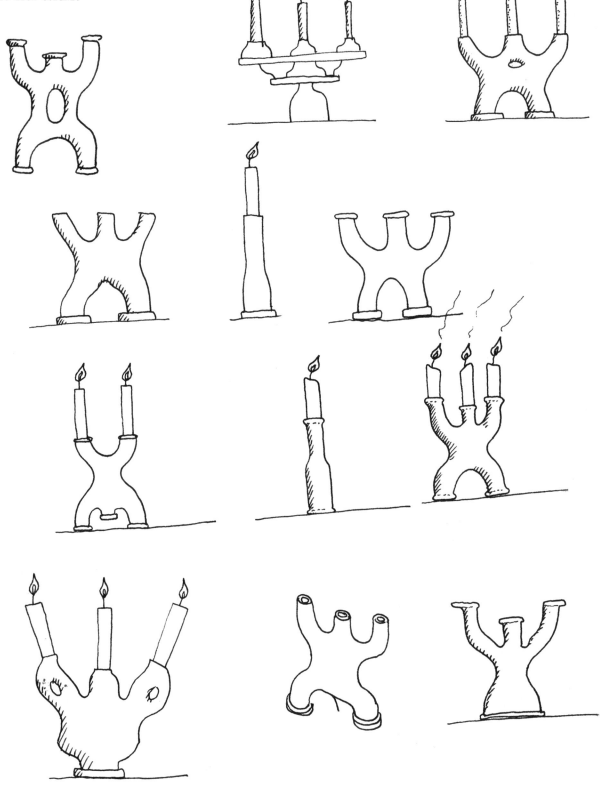

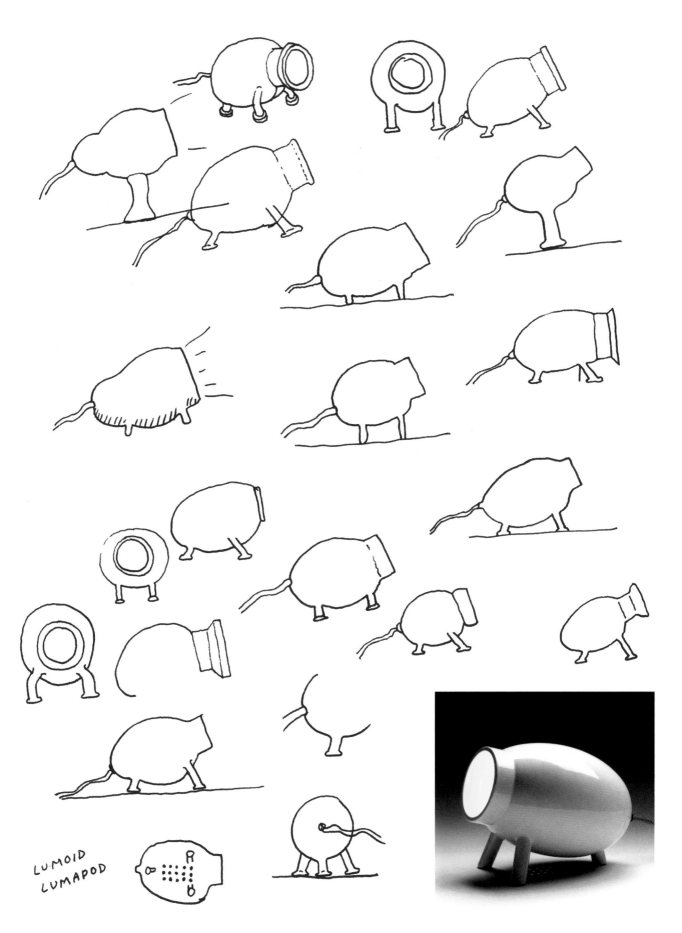

LUMOID
LUMAPOD

A series of designs for household objects including rugs, doormats and tablecloths

"DOOR MAT"
006

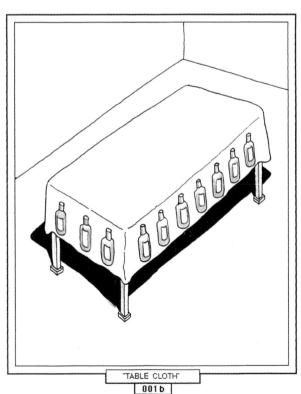

"TABLE CLOTH"
001b

"PROGETTO"
"HONG KONG"
DESIGN
GALLERY
MILANO

TABLECLOTHS
NAPKINS
TABLE LIGHTERS
MINI BAR
TELEPHONE TABLE
CARPETS

"CARPET"
005

CITIZEN OFFICE EXHIBITION, VITRA • 1992

The overriding thought that emerged during the discussion
meetings was that of a 'plural approach' to the functional
and non-functional themes of the environment. This idea
developed into the separation of the working environment
into specific areas of research. Each diagram has been
designed to represent a 'zone', within which it is
possible to reflect upon, and study products without the
pressure of the 'total'.

The aim was to create a space that is no longer total,
but plural, responsive, flexible, humanistic and
qualitatively superior. An environment capable of
absorbing, changing and aging, of being content and yet,
non-conformative, so as to inspire the individual to
determine for themselves how they live, work, relate and
relax. - James Irvine

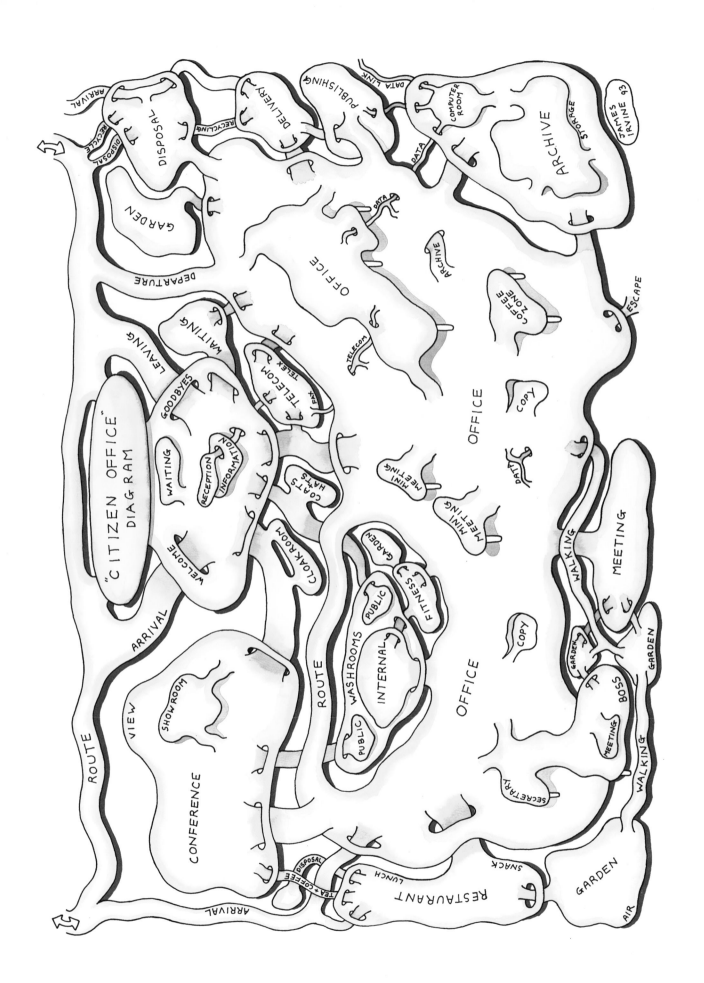

MICHELE DE LUCCHI

A PORTRAIT IN POST-MEMPHIS MILAN

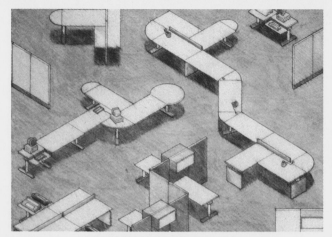

Irvine's sketch for the Delphos office system designed by Ettore Sottsass and Michele De Lucchi with Irvine for Olivetti Synthesis, 1985

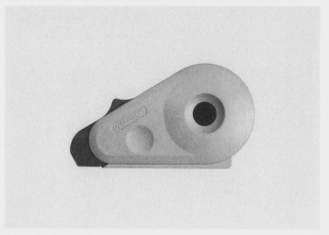

Paper On-Paper Stick office stationery designed by Michele De Lucchi with Irvine for Olivetti, 1991

FRANCESCA PICCHI: From 1984 you worked as a consultant responsible for all Olivetti's products at Ivrea, until in 1992 Sottsass put you in charge of the company. James himself arrived in Milan in 1984. How does he come into this story?

MICHELE DE LUCCHI: I'm not entirely sure, but I think I was the first person he got to know when he arrived in Italy. As we know, at Olivetti, design was never a department within the company, because it was seen as the discipline whose function was to bring together the world of industrial technology (tightly focused on manufacturing and innovation) and that of human beings: everyday life and the wildest, most fantastic desires and dreams. On that basis, the company was organized in such a way that that communications and design were a single department. I couldn't explain why that was, but it worked. It was as if that unified department represented the company's cultured 'soul', thanks also to those who headed it, the extraordinary intellectuals Renzo Zorzi and Paolo Viti.

Communications was famous for organizing highly sophisticated exhibitions that attracted wide attention in the media. They included one on the restoration of Cimabue's *Crucifixion*, damaged in the Florence floods of 1966, and another on the horses of San Marco, in Venice. James's father was an architect and he was known around Olivetti because he had organized that exhibition in London. Links of that sort were behind James's move to Milan.

One day, Paolo Viti called me to say, 'Let me introduce your new assistant.' That's how James and I started working together. Our first joint project was the Delphos system for Olivetti Synthesis (the office furniture division). We had to go back and forth between Milan and Massa Carrara, where the factory was, two or three times a week. His Italian wasn't great then, and in exchange I learned English; in fact, what I know, I learned from him on those frequent long car journeys. Later on we designed various machines together: printers, keyboards, fax machines and so on. Olivetti's design office was in Milan, on the Corso Venezia, and Ettore Sottsass, Mario Bellini, Antonio Macchi Cassia and George Sowden all gravitated towards it.

FP: How do you see James's contribution to your designs for Olivetti?

MDL: I could say I recognize James's hand in a certain roundness and softness in the shapes we were designing at that time – non-aggressive shapes: for example, a small stationery object like Paper On-Paper Stick; James's hand is clearly visible there.

FP: Where?

MDL: Everywhere. Including the name. If you look closely, you can see the reference to the form of a duck. James had a highly developed sense of irony. It was in his character, and he tried to put aspects of his own behaviour into the objects he designed.

FP: His training as a product designer specializing in advanced technical products continued at Olivetti and had very interesting results when he went to Japan

CARO GIEIMS

QUI VA TUTTO BENE. È ARRIVATA L'ESTATE
E ABBIAMO INCOMINCIATO A MANGIARE GLI SPAGHETTI
CON IL PEPERONCINO. MOLTO MOLTO PICCANTI. —
L'ARCHITETTURA E IL DESIGN SONO ANCORA
MOLTO SERI E SEVERI : NON SIAMO ANCORA
RIUSCITI A DIVENTARE AMICI MA CI RIUSCIREMO
PRESTO. —
MANGIA TANTO SUSHI
SALUTI DA
ZIO MICHELE

Letter from De Lucchi to Irvine during his time in Japan for the Toshiba Olivetti exchange, 1987

to work for Toshiba. Don't you think that by staying in Italy James was penalized, in that after his time with Olivetti he almost exclusively designed furniture?

MDL: The concept for a computer that he developed in Japan and seemed to anticipate something like the iPad that came much later, shows me very clearly that James would have been an ideal designer for a company like Apple, except that in Italy at that time we weren't developing the technology; that was the real limitation. It could be said that precisely because of his good fortune in coming to Milan, James suffered the disadvantage of not finding himself in an innovative technological environment where his contribution could have been much more highly valued.

Over the past few years we met infrequently, but I followed his work and I could spot it anywhere. James was always very consistent in his designs, his thinking and the way in which he visualized things. He was never swayed by trends or fashions. That overall clarity is reflected in the way he produced

designs with a very well-defined outline, as if he always wanted things to have a perimeter. If you look closely at his designs, they have very gentle, rounded shapes – the kind he liked.

FP: Speaking of his way of drawing, with clean lines and without corrections, Jasper Morrison describes how one of the games they played when they were students at the Royal College of Art was to challenge each other not to take their pen off the paper, and to design an object with a single continuous line.

MDL: James left nothing to chance: his drawings were always finished and complete. Very often, you can see in the lines of a drawing the designer's first thoughts and revisions, but he was so precise that he even drew the space round objects, an approach he had learned from Ettore. In fact, in those years I recall a certain commonality of vision between Ettore and James.

FP: Not long after he arrived in Milan, James became immersed in what Andrea Branzi calls 'a strange

Citizen Office exhibition for Vitra, Basel, 1991 (L-R: Andrea Branzi, Michele De Lucchi, Ettore Sottsass, James Irvine)

of design, we had invited a group of young Italian comic-strip artists.

FP: It seems to me that at a certain point you were faced with the problem of knowing what would happen after Memphis. Memphis had attempted to create a new relationship with industry following the Radical experiment that had rejected such a thing, and tried out more basic, direct methods and a return to craftsmanship, but for designers of James's generation, industry was the central issue. They looked for direct links with that rich network of small family-owned factories so typical of Italian manufacturing but neglected by the big names, in a spirit you might call a little romantic.

MDL: I would say, rather, that Memphis had tried to establish a critical relationship with industry. In general, I think it can be put like this: James always wanted to design 'products', not art objects for an intellectual elite. He was interested in the product as a consumer object. It must be said that at the time, great emphasis was placed on the distinction between designs and products, in the sense that designs did not necessarily have to become mass-market products. Designs were seen as a means of influencing and guiding the public and making it self-critical.

FP: I believe that the need to cultivate the experimental, collective aspects of design profoundly influenced James's view of the industry. But something that has always struck me is that although, as his business partner, he could have spoken Sottsass's language – the famous 'Sotts-Art' of which Branzi speaks – in fact he always steered clear of it.

MDL: James was always true to James. His touch can always be recognized. Even his most visionary works have a logical clarity. His training was pragmatic, highly empirical, but he had an extraordinary ability to organize information logically and systematically. I recall that for the Citizen Office project for Vitra, of which he was overall coordinator, James made a very beautiful drawing: a sort of big stomach surrounded by a tangle of intestines capable of describing analytically and very clearly how all the functions would relate to each other.

FP: In 1986 you organized 'Solid: A new collection of objects for the home', and you invited James to

mixture of radicalism and high-end product design'. It is significant that in that same year, 1986, he designed the Delphos office system and took part in a Memphis exhibition.

MDL: When he arrived in Milan, James had just graduated from the RCA. I think his encounter with the world of Milan was in a way a shock, and perhaps a liberation too. Those were years in which there was a real split in the things we were doing. We were completely taken up by the contrast between Olivetti – which meant big numbers, market values, production, marketing, sales – in a word, 'industry' – and the experimental, totally abstract, revolutionary, avant-garde world of Memphis and post-Memphis.
James took part in the 'Twelve New' exhibition, which was one of the last Memphis exhibitions. At that time we felt a very strong desire to create a fusion with the new tendencies that were emerging; we were especially interested in different modes of figuration and communication. In an effort to broaden Memphis's range of references, which were rooted in the world

participate. It occurs to me that this kind of collective experiment was in some way a precursor of Progetto Oggetto, the project that James and Jasper Morrison devised for Cappellini a few years later. I feel the experience of Solid was central, because it included thoughts about objects for everyday use: the sort of attention that had become lost in the large sculptural objects of Sottsass and Memphis. Solid also seemed to distance itself from Memphis and declare itself critical of it. It struck me, for example, that you stated that 'the explosion of decoration of the early 1980s was now exhausted'.

MDL: Solid certainly expressed the desire to go beyond Memphis. The opportunity was created by a Bergamo industrialist, the owner of Rossana RB kitchens. Owning so many outlets, he experienced the problem of dressing his window displays and differentiating himself from his competitors. On the basis of that request we adopted the idea of designing very small decorative objects: things for the table and the home.

But we held the first exhibition in an art gallery, Studio Marconi, and I don't believe any of those objects ever appeared in a showroom. They were experiments that made us feel that something different was coming into being, or at least that Memphis had sown a seed here and there. We chose the name 'Solid' because it was a word that could be understood in every language, and we wanted to cultivate that international dimension. After Memphis, we wanted to express the idea of being solid and concrete.

FP: In that case, can it be seen as a reaction to Memphis?

MDL: More than a reaction, it was of kind of test to see how the Memphis experiment could be continued and taken forward. In 1987, the year of Solid, we had decided to say the Memphis experiment had come to an end, and we already felt a bit like survivors. It was only the end of the 1980s, but we were determined to take every possible opportunity to return to that experimental situation.

The idea of being able to do things without a commercial brief, not having to make products for specific niches in the market, with predetermined qualities and materials, was the motive for our going in search of what we could do that was new and different. In the Solid range of products there are many ceramic objects, including some vases designed

The Solid team, 1986 (L-R: Nick Bewick, Angelo Micheli, Mathilde Bretillot, Geert Koster, Christian Hartmaan, James Irvine, Simon Morgan)

by James; who would ever have thought we would be designing ceramics for industry?

FP: In the text you wrote for the presentation of Solid you put geometry at the centre of your formal research: it was used in an almost anti-decorative way. While the Memphis manner was to use free and strong decoration, you seem to have adopted a compositional approach based on dismantling and reassembling forms. That freedom and articulation of formal elements is especially evident in James's designs, which express that intention to create free, almost unstable constructions with a strong figurative component. It is a compositional approach that is very different from what later became his distinctive style with its very clear formal syntheses.

MDL: You're right, breaking down and reassembling elements was typical of those years. Remember, we were strongly influenced by Ettore's personality – I myself was enthralled by his charisma for a very long time – and so we looked to him and what he was doing. We all worked with primary forms and colour derived from his compositional method. Ettore worked through addition. Unlike the deconstructivists, he added to the construction, rather than breaking it down. For example, he would start by drawing a cube – a primary form – and then gradually add to it, and we did that, too.

I couldn't say now exactly when we felt it consciously, but our real concern, especially when the forms were over-simplified, was to express something very powerful in the detail, in pursuit of subtle

Portaoggetti, a ceramic storage tray for Solid, 1986

elegance. Most of the time we achieved the effect of detail by two means: on the one hand decoration, and on the other the articulation of forms. James, for example, always worked on the articulation of forms. Remember that for us, decoration had become a fundamental element of our thinking. It wasn't simply a texture to be applied over a form; rather, we started from decoration and then proceeded to the formal construction.

James, of course, wasn't affected by all that. In fact, I can't remember his creating any decoration. His designs for Solid confirm that in most cases he used the material to create the sense of a unique, finished object. I recall that he designed beautiful ceramics in which the material was used for what it could do. And ceramic worked very well in James's mind, because it's a material that accepts the rotundity and softness that James felt was his hallmark. On the other hand, he felt nothing at all for laminated plastic, which was at the centre of experimentation in those years.

FP: I'm perhaps struck by the drawings produced for Solid even more forcefully than by the objects that were made. In James's archive I found a great quantity of drawings labelled 'Solid' in many different techniques, from wax crayon and watercolour to black-and-white ink sketches.

MDL: Drawing was at the centre of the world to which Sottsass, Memphis and experiments like Solid belonged. We all did it. Ettore, for example, would go home at six and draw late into the night. And for James, too, drawings were the beginning of everything. The design started with the drawing. The idea never came first and the drawing second. His drawings show how the design could be more like a logical consequence, a continuous thread controlled with great precision. He hardly ever did the sort of doodles you play around with while you're talking. His drawings were accurate and precise, already part of a detailed formal composition based on symmetry or the composition of masses, sometimes with a frame that held everything together on the page. The idea wasn't that the drawing was a preparatory element that would disappear as soon as the object was made: it had the same value as the final product.

FP: Do you think it's possible to identify a link between Solid and a project like Progetto Oggetto? I think both of them were looking for a certain classicism in design that would also take into account everything that had happened before: a kind of determination to create contemporary classics.

MDL: You're referring to a presumed classicism, but I would rather call it 'plasticity', in the sense of not being afraid to talk about form. We had cultivated a kind of reverence for form. Perhaps because there had been that Radical world that put everything up for discussion and challenged everything. The project itself was seen as a form of violence against the world because it tended to infringe upon personal freedom.

It was that position that led me to demonstrate outside the Triennale, dressed as a general. I was trying to embody a metaphor according to which the designer, like a general, imposes his own rules and designs. And when he imposes his form, he imposes the behaviour those forms imply, and thus he exerts some kind of power on the world of which he is entirely unaware. The whole Radical world was moving in that direction because it put at the centre the question of the designer's role in society.

FP: I'd like to conclude by returning to the climate that prevailed around design in Milan in the years after Memphis. I've often wondered why design was so important. My impression is that it represented a whole system of thought, something so important for society and the world.

MDL: It was like being part of a huge, unique challenge to the world, and everyone was ready to enter the fray.

Irvine at the drawing table in De Lucchi's office, Milan, 1984

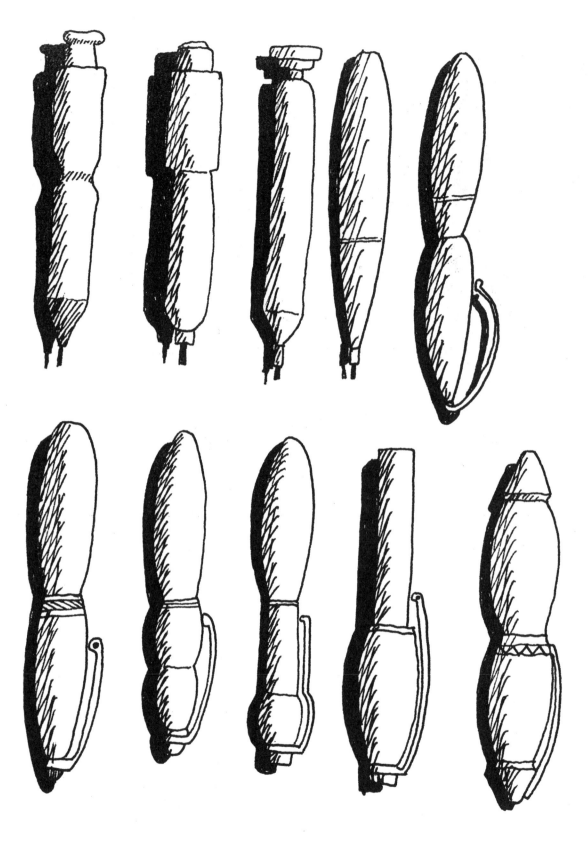

PENS + PENCILS.

GEORGE SOWDEN

AVOIDING SHARP EDGES

The Milan-based Olivetti team, 1985 (back row L-R: Antonio Macchi Cassia, Michele De Lucchi, Ettore Sottsass, Adolfo Della Thea, Theo Gonser, Eric Gottiem; front row L-R: James Irvine, Simon Morgan, Geroge Sowden, Marco Susani)

FRANCESCA PICCHI: You were one of the first to meet James when he arrived in Milan.

GEORGE SOWDEN: I met James when he arrived to work at Olivetti. He had just graduated from the Royal College of Art in London. At that time Ettore Sottsass had put together a working team at Olivetti and Michele De Lucchi and I were among his closest collaborators. However, two distinct currents formed within this team: Michele and James on one side, and on the other myself and Simon Morgan (a young Englishman who had studied at the RCA with James and whom James met again in Milan). This division into two groups created an interesting work dynamic at Olivetti.

So, I knew James from about 1984 onwards. Our close friendship, however, dated to the time James left Sottsass Associati. Over the following years we got to

know each other better, and shared confidences and anecdotes. James loved telling stories and discussing harmless gossip. Our relationship became closer later, during the last years of his life. Jasper, Stefano, Joel and I were the only ones with whom he talked about his illness. He made us promise we wouldn't breathe a word about it to anyone, and that's what we did. James was very discreet and courageous. And he didn't want his illness to affect his work and his relationships with others.

FP: In your discussions, what were the subjects that you got most into?

GS: We didn't talk so much about design – we enjoyed telling each other stories and sharing snippets of news. James was a great raconteur and told wonderful tales. They sounded new every time: he was very entertaining.

I remember, for example, the story of how he had been punished at school. He was about nine years old. One morning, walking to school with his father, they saw that the pavement in front of the entrance was being laid with fresh concrete. James said goodbye to his father and went in. Halfway through the morning he was summoned to the headmaster's office because someone had carved the initials 'JI' into the wet cement. Right away he was suspected of being the culprit and was asked to confess. He knew nothing about it but he was caned twice: once for the deed itself, and the second time for not owning up and therefore, presumably lying.

When his father got home, seeing the bruises, he was so furious he consulted a lawyer and, in order to document what had happened, he took a photo of James and sent it to the press. The *Guardian* newspaper published it on its front page. That photo became one of the key points in the debate about the abolition of corporal punishment in British schools. James's bum on the front page! That fact continued to amuse him greatly. But what amused him most of all was the fact that it had been his father who had written in the wet concrete as a surprise for his son.

FP: Both you and James, being British, share not only a certain type of training, but also a love for Milan that led you to stay and live in the city.

GS: I came to Milan looking for work, but also looking for something I hadn't found in England — I wanted to find better reasons for doing the job I had chosen, reasons unlike the pragmatic or rational ones I found at home. In England I didn't find much that fulfilled me; in Italy I found lots of new things interesting. I remember that when I first met Ettore Sottsass and showed him my drawings he was very complimentary. It was in his office that I began to discover the anthropological, psychological, poetic and emotional aspect of our work. I think James, too, found in Milan a congenial environment, open, vibrant and welcoming, where he was able to grow.

FP: Can you explain why you both decided to put down roots in Milan?

GS: I arrived in Milan in the 1970s, and James some time later, in the 1980s. In those days Milan was an extraordinary place. You only had to go to the Brianza region to find highly skilled artisans who were prepared to experiment. It wouldn't have been possible in Britain where craftsmanship had been unsupported and allowed to disappear. The direct contact with making things was fantastic, watching things happen. Designing, after all, is a craft. Milan was very different then. There was great freedom, respect for creativity and recognition of the economic possibilities coming out of it.

FP: I was always struck by James's relationship with Ettore Sottsass. While 'legitimated', so to speak, by his status as partner, James never 'reworked' Sottsass or used an idiom 'à la Sottsass'. Despite the fact that James's more formal world was in many ways far from Ettore's, it is also true that they shared a very clear, simple, ordered vision.

GS: What you learned from Sottsass was not a style but an attitude: you learned to find your own way and of all the people close to him, James is one of those who achieved this. He 'reworked' Sottsass in the sense that he repeated the same journey, building references and structuring his own ideals. By the time James arrived in Milan, none of us, from Sottsass down, believed in absolute values any more. James, too, quickly embraced the openness towards individual expression and was skillful in finding his own place. He completely understood Ettore's attitude. I'm sure James learned a great deal being close to him.

In addition, James had the wonderful opportunity of working at Olivetti; learning about manufacturing and, like me, getting to know industrial processes and how they worked. I'm sure that even as a child he knew how to assemble things, how to take them apart and how to re-build them — he was good at it — motor bikes for example. But what he learned from the engineers at Olivetti was that making things involves specific processes and how design fitted into them. Processes difficult to understand today because it's no longer possible to have this kind of hands-on experience in manufacturing. I believe that one of the reasons why so many young designers become artists is that, having never worked in a manufacturing context, they don't know or understand the complexities of putting things into production. James, however, knew it very well and it is evident in his work.

FP: How would you describe his formal vision?

GS: James and I shared a love of soft forms, the kind that are nice to touch when you come into contact with them, and if you think that way you tend to avoid sharp edges.

FP: As you say, James was passionate about the way things worked. He liked taking apart and reassembling all sorts of things, an aptitude he had from childhood, so much so that his mother describes how in the park, while other children were happily playing, he enjoyed taking his pram apart. I believe the same passion was at the core of his love of manufacturing and design.

GS: British people are mechanically minded, you know. Just think about the industrial revolution of the 1800s. It's in our DNA, our culture. One of the great stories of our industrial history is the nineteenth-century boom of the railway industry. I doubt that there is a single British boy of James's generation or mine who hasn't played with a model train set. Bridges, locomotives and railways are part of our everyday landscape. If you grow up in such a society, such an environment, you're likely to have traces of that sensitivity towards all things mechanical left in you. And, importantly, when talking about design, we need to remember that mechanical things have an intrinsic aesthetic quality, which is inescapable. James had the chance to know and understand what it means.

Also, if we consider that during James's London Royal College days, 'high-tech' was the aesthetic byword, and that his first job after the RCA was in Norman Foster's studio, we can understand that James received very powerful input. Those were the years when London saw its first buildings, which displayed bolts, pipes and inner structures in full view, and maybe high-tech is the ultimate expression of the aesthetics of the machine.

However, James, like many of us, found himself experiencing the transition from a mechanical to an electronic world first hand, from the inside and as an industrial designer, working for one of the leading manufacturers of communication devices — making decisions during this transition was felt more sharply, and it was not easy, as we had a foot on both sides of the fence.

FP: Do you think, then, that James's predisposition for logical and comprehensible forms was influenced by that experience of mechanics?

GS: As I said, mechanical things have a strong intrinsic aesthetic of their own, (a bicycle is always a bicycle however it is designed) while electronic things have none at all. This means that that when designing electronic objects we work in the realm of what I call applied aesthetics. It was during this period of transition from mechanical to electronic products, that we also found a growing consciousness marking the shift from modernist ideology to post-modern thinking. Applied aesthetics began turning up everywhere — in the 1980s, when designers realized that electronic devices could assume any look, things like telephones shaped as a banana began to arrive on the market. The jokes eventually became stale but applied aesthetics are now the norm and have become very sophisticated.

FP: Despite the fact that in the 1980s, technology involved bulky components and a certain typological rigidity, in the computer concept that James designed for Toshiba in 1987 while in Japan on the Olivetti–Toshiba cultural exchange, he displayed a much freer, more relaxed vision of the technological object: the computer almost resembles an iPad. Don't you think the discussions held at Olivetti influenced that vision?

GS: I love that design: we could say that it's ahead of its time, beautiful. It's difficult to say what James had in mind: it anticipated many other things — Apple, for instance, in 1987 wasn't anywhere near that kind solution. In terms of technology, I don't know where he got the idea from, there wasn't much around, but I don't think it came from Olivetti.

The experience at Olivetti did, however, give him the opportunity to understand from the inside the rules and limits of a way of foreseeing and handling industrial production processes through which you might project the future.

FP: When James arrived at Olivetti you were already fully involved in a process of change destined to impact on people's perception of the everyday environment. You and Michele De Lucchi, in particular, working alongside Sottsass, found yourselves living at the end of one epoch and the beginning of another — the mechanical age was becoming the electronic age and linked with electronic technology and its apparent formal 'freedom'. In particular, you and Sottsass designed the first electronic machines in Europe.

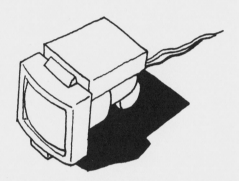

Sketch for 10-inch television for Toshiba, 1987

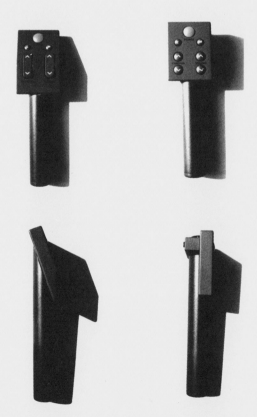

Remote control for 10-inch television for Toshiba, 1987

Can you tell us about it?

GS: As far as my experience is concerned, I can say that when I started working on electronics, the first computers were essentially typewriters where the sheet of paper had been replaced by huge cathode tubes. All this meant considerable bulk and unmanageable size; we turned to ergonomics for help to find a way to use these things. Today it may be difficult to understand the complexity of the technical problems we were facing; over time everything has become simplified and much smaller. Maybe it is enough to say, for example, that each single key on a keyboard in the 1970s was an extremely complicated mechanical device. However, the enormous technological changes that were about to happen because of electronics, meant all aspects of the design process would never be the same again – and we have to include Memphis in this epochal moment.

FP: I think that the huge impact that Memphis has had on visual idioms has not been fully recognised, and to some extent is even misunderstood, especially in Italy. Its huge impact on visual form has never been recognized. The type of experience that welcomes diversity – the cross-pollination of widely different things – started with Memphis. The idiom of historic avant-gardes was challenged and infiltrated by elements of Pop culture represented by everyday objects such as the plastic laminate tables of milk bars or the blotched pages of the ledgers in public offices. I'm keen to understand what you think, and how you think Memphis got under James's skin, into his formal world, given that in a way he contributed to its being overtaken by the success of his own generation.

GS: In the context of technological changes, we should add that Memphis happened during the same simultaneous watershed moment of change between mechanical/electronic and modernism/post-modernism – the early 1980s. For me the problem is very simple: by the 1970s modernism had become a dogma, a fundamentalist ideology controlled by an academic apparatus that left little space for any stylistic experiments; (even style was a dirty word).
    Notions of what was good design had been codified and anything outside the code was condemned and excluded. What Memphis succeeded in doing was to open a door waiting to be opened – it was inevitable and necessary at the same time.

GEORGE SOWDEN

Catalogue for the 'Dodici Nuovi - Twelve New' Memphis exhibition, 1986

Things had to happen. What had been blocked and paralysed needed to be prised open again and Memphis was an amazing, liberating shared event that managed to do it. The British critic Jonathan Glancey wrote, with a worried tone, that Memphis was pernicious – of course, he was absolutely right in the sense that modernism, as an ideal, would collapse under the weight. People often ask me about Memphis, talking about it in terms of style.

Even today it is misunderstood as such. But, Memphis was the result of a change of attitude – I remember when Ettore asked Dieter Rams to design something for Memphis. Rams was surprised and asked: 'But what should I do? I'm not able to design in that style.' Ettore replied, 'Just do what you do, that's more than enough, you don't have to do anything differently.' Sottsass had asked Rams because he believed him to be a very sensitive spokesman of design and, after all, Memphis had pushed design to become a form of individual communication.

Put it this way, if you are confined to designing something that represents an academic ideal, it's very different from doing something personal that communicates a poetic idea – both Rams and Sottsass designed this personal way – a similar poetic journey, different poetic values!

FP: It seems to me, though, that James, through his proximity to Sottsass and his participation in one of the last Memphis events (the 'Twelve New' exhibition) had absorbed the themes of that intellectual and emotional tension, had made them his own and in some way had disseminated them amongst the new generation of designers that emerged in the 1990s. Paradoxically, however, this new generation was perceived as championing a return to order, as acting to restore the modernist movement, and was supported by that very academic world that had refused to open itself to any 'contamination' and had tried to build a barrier against the contemporary world. I'd like to ask you whether you share that view.

GS: I think that what this new generation did was in any case post-modern. Memphis had been so outrageous that everybody was forced to reposition him or herself in relationship to it. But what James, Jasper Morrison and their group of friends did was not re-establish order but, towards the end of the 1980s, communicate something significantly different and particularly relevant at the time by adopting a language that expressed simplicity. With the fragmentation of ideology that happened during the 1980s, it was inevitable that the results of design activity would become a non-idealistic 'collage' with an infinite number of ideas. This is the situation today and the collage is ever changing.

FP: So do you think that James, too, was post-modern?

GS: Of course he was, he couldn't have been anything else. Even though he was fond of the poetics of 'beautiful modern', I simply believe that his sensitivity didn't particularly lean towards complexity – unlike mine. However, James was himself and it would be now pointless to label him. He was an individualist who pushed his sensitivity to the limit; and he was very good. Looking at his drawings from the late 1980s we can see he'd already gone beyond modernism.

His designs for the Solid project, for example, aren't at all modernist; instead they represent an experimental phase where he himself was trying to reposition his work – even vis-à-vis Memphis, which was still an ever-present phenomenon. His designs of that period belong to a process of aesthetic research that slowly resolved itself as he found his own personal place. The 1980s were wild. Memphis had set the cat among the pigeons and had changed everything.

As far as I'm concerned it was a time of irrepressible energy and restlessness. At one point we probably felt the need to slow down.

This was the context for the appearance of the young British designers of James's generation, who met at Cappellini – yes, it was them that halted the tsunami for a while and it's also true that they momentarily expressed a kind of new visual order.

FP: With Progetto Oggetto, curated for Cappellini by James and Jasper Morrison, a generation of designers emerged, with different histories and geographical backgrounds, but on the same formal wavelength. All of them asserted the aesthetic of simplicity. This response came from James himself, who knew the elements in question very well, having been part of that period at Memphis, if only peripherally. What do you think?

GS: The way I see it, Progetto Oggetto started with the idea of simplicity, but yet very far from an attempted restoration of modernism. When you start a new project any designer takes a stance. One of the problems of individuality in design is to decide what your attitude is because it will be that which points you in a particular direction. Ideology can do that for you but then you need to believe in it, which is quite difficult these days.

FP: James believed design could make the world a better place?

GS: Certainly. He also had an acute sensibility. And he adored his job. I think today with the vast quantity of goods being produced we no longer have a clue about what is good or bad design. If we think of all the very successful objects that are produced in huge numbers, we get the strange feeling that they represent good design because they are sold by the millions every year, but can we say that this invasive omnipresence of something is a good or a bad thing?

As it happens, I believe another fundamental repositioning is underway, where it isn't the aesthetic quality of an object that is important, but what that object represents. Nobody can claim that a machine gun is not well designed – the problem is what you do with it. Same with SUVs, extraordinary objects, but why do we need them? I remember, back in the 1970s Sottsass used to exclaim: 'Coca Cola, a fantastic product, but a lousy drink!' I realize this is a very

difficult time for designers. We are caught up in the idea of adding something successful to the excess of objects already existing in the world. Maybe it is time for a change?

FP: I'm sure that to describe a creative person one must dig into his or her beginnings, because that's where you find all the elements (both developed and discarded) needed to understand the path he or she has subsequently followed. In this sense the experiments of the late 1980s are crucial for an understanding of James's journey. In general, how do you think one should read the research represented by James's designs of that period – the sketches, the pastels, the watercolours for Solid, or his other experiences?

GS: The designs from that period are poetic gestures, experiments. All designers need to find their points of reference. We have created an opportunity to be free from ideologies, and therefore we now need to understand how to manage this freedom. A society without reference points is very difficult to manage, it needs to be extremely democratic and tolerant. However, it's clear that his drawings from the 1980s are part of an experimental journey that made James into who he was. At some point he found a way of expressing perfectly his sensibility and his interests. The drawings reveal the search for a language that he was involved in at that time. It's through drawing that we put other things into focus.

FP: To conclude, I'd like to ask you if you saw a formal development in James's work.

GS: Despite everything, James always wanted to believe in design and I think he had a clear idea of what he thought to be correct. He had a strong moral sense and feeling of responsibility toward the planet. He was definitely not frivolous. I think that latterly he was widening the range of his personal spectrum with a precise idea of what the world needed, visually. He was in tune. He knew exactly what he didn't want to do – he hated waste and pollution.

GIULIO CAPPELLINI

CROSS-POLLINATION DESIGN

FRANCESCA PICCHI: The Cappellini brand played a crucial role in the late 1980s and early 1990s. It was central to that moment of renewal, bringing together a group of young designers from diverse geographical and cultural backgrounds, all sharing what I would call a 'classic' approach to design.

GIULIO CAPPELLINI: It's a period that has still not been explored in depth: it was a moment of great change, but we didn't realize that at the time.

FP: James Irvine and Jasper Morrison could be said to have been at the centre of that circle of young designers. How did you all meet?

GC: It was completely by chance. I had recently started working with Jasper, whom I had met in London at the time of Aram's twenty-fifth anniversary. Jasper was a good friend of James, and used to stay with him when he was in Milan. I recall that early one morning I went to pick up Jasper to take him to my office in Brianza. James, clearly thinking I was someone else, casually opened the door in boxer shorts and a T-shirt, and he was a little disconcerted at seeing me. I hardly said hello because no sooner had he opened the door than I caught sight of the prototype of a chair at the end of the hallway, and so, almost without looking at him, I went straight for the cardboard model. It was the first prototype of the Piceno chair, which was put into production by Cappellini and was in our collection for many years. From that first, very informal meeting sprang a strong professional and personal relationship.

FP: The Piceno chair marked a turning point in James's career: it was his first chair. And that story demonstrates James's admiration for the spontaneity of Italian industrialists, who could fall in love with a design to the point of wanting to produce it no matter what the cost, and regardless of marketing logic.

GC: In fact, I was stunned by the Piceno: it was a huge challenge. It was the fruit of a very intensive search for sophisticated quality in manufacture. I was struck by the use of plywood in the design, and the way it was allied to traditional ways of working with wood, even in their expressive aspects. Laminate is a material that in the history of design has always involved the idea of production in series – one need only think of the pressed wood chairs designed by

Alvar Aalto and Charles and Ray Eames. And I was struck by the care with which James had designed the details, working together with the manufacturers. The layer of felt for the seat – which gave the chair a splash of colour – was made by a company with a long history, the last one in Europe to produce felt of that thickness.

FP: In 1992, James, with Jasper Morrison, launched the collective project Progetto Oggetto. How did it come into being?

GC: I should first say that in those years post-modernism and, perhaps even more, the figure of Ettore Sottsass – with his Superboxes, and his extraordinary altar-like furniture and large-scale ceramics – had led to the preference for large, sculptural objects. I felt there was a gap in the market for small objects, which in some way were part of the post-war Italian tradition of 'form of the useful', and that it had to be filled. So I turned to Jasper and James and told them I would like to create a series of objects, functional or otherwise, for everyday use. We started working on it, but it was a bit of a 'Sunday' project, in the sense that we spent our free time on it. The first task was to make a list of people we'd like to involve.

As I said, I thought it would be interesting to revive the notion of designing objects for everyday use, which in the 1950s had produced some remarkable results but had then got somewhat lost. At that time, in the late 1980s and early 1990s, the preference was for large objects, furniture especially, and the whole world of ordinary things had almost been forgotten.

So we devoted ourselves to that idea, seeing it as a team project, almost an experiment in cross-disciplinary design. James (from Milan) and Jasper (from London) coordinated everything. The basis of the project was to involve different people from all over the world, responsible for history, culture, or tradition: the approach was deliberately international and global. We decided to give them great freedom in terms of the product, use of materials, and technology, but above all in how they expressed themselves: respect for each person's individual vision was extremely important. And in any case, when we launched Progetto Oggetto we were drawn to the idea of diversity rather than the expression of a single idiom. We were interested in creating a multifaceted idiom that would express the differing visions of individuals with their different approaches to objects.

Sketches for the Piceno collection, 1991

That balance was not easily achieved, and credit must be given to James and Jasper for their ability to hold all that complexity together with great generosity and a clear vision. We knew we were running the risk of presenting a chaotic, incomprehensible project, ragged at the edges, since the bold aim of backing a 'multicultural' project also demanded a certain degree of consistency among the objects produced.

Now it feels as if it was really easy. Above all, I realize that the pace now is entirely different from what it was then. I recall that we held our first meetings with James and Jasper at Lake Como. They would come to Brianza by train, and I would meet them at the station at Carugo and take them down to the lake. We'd find a little trattoria – we usually went out of season, in the autumn, and there were few people about. We'd have lunch and begin our long meetings, full of discussion, which went on after lunch and finished on a bench in a small square, where we would sit and argue and put together our ideas about what was to become Progetto Oggetto. It makes me smile now to describe that little scene, but that's how it was.

FP: All that talk surprises me: Jasper Morrison is known to not particularly like talking, to the point of calling his first book *A World Without Words*. And James never liked to acknowledge his skill in bringing people together and acting as a catalyst.

GC: Actually, the collective concept was very important to all of us, and James in particular – he sometimes pursued it at the expense of his own individuality. In his dealings with others, James displayed extraordinary generosity, and frequently preferred to stay in the background. The example of Progetto Oggetto clearly shows him in that light: when he first asked if he could create a collection of objects, he could have decided to design them himself, and then submit his proposals to me. Instead, he and Jasper insisted on a collaborative project. That collective spirit applied to every aspect of Progetto Oggetto, from the choice of designers to the designs and their presentation, the catalogues and the exhibitions. We also created a sort of little selection committee to choose which objects we should produce. It worked freely and instinctively, without our knowing who had designed what.

That was a time when group work was in vogue. A new generation of designers was emerging; they were to become international stars but felt the need for generous communication with their fellow designers. James really had that kind of generosity. Everyone spoke his own design language, but together they expressed a profound need for debate and reflection as an important stage in the design project. That's an attitude we've definitely lost over the years. Thinking back, I realize we speak less as time goes on, our meetings are often hurried and we no longer find time to sit down and think in a more systematic way. But in those days that way of pondering and discussing was entirely natural, almost a habit we felt at ease with.

FP: Progetto Oggetto and your work at Cappellini had a 'collateral effect' that influenced design and its associated rituals. Would you agree that the

GIULIO CAPPELLINI

Progetto Oggetto presentation at the Cappellini showroom in Carugo, 1992

conversation with a series of virtual ones drawn on the walls to represent elements of interior architecture, providing a background for the objects.

It's true that this kind of freedom of action was unprecedented. The Fiera was a catalyst for all the energies associated with design, and these events were also successful because nothing of the kind had been done anywhere in the city. The shows were an important means of communication. We later presented Progetto Oggetto at Documenta 8, in Kassel, one of the first attempts to 'contaminate' art with design. Alongside that culturally ambitious experiment we designed shop windows for the Liberty store, in London, in a decidedly more commercial style.

FP: Cappellini was the 'place' where James and Jasper designed many products together, but the only one that was produced under their joint names was Alfabeto System, a home storage system they designed in 1996.

GC: The idea behind Alfabeto System was to create an inexpensive shelving and storage system, but our distributors turned it down. I thought it made sense to make a product that would appeal to young people, but the marketing department didn't have faith in it. With its use of laminate and natural wood trim, and its extreme plainness and simplicity, it was ahead of its time and did not appeal to contemporary taste. And in any case, the market isn't always right: for instance, to begin with, we sold only three examples of Jasper's Thinking Man's Chair, one of our best long-term sellers. A product sometimes needs time to be properly understood.

FP: In those years industry was again part of the design myth for the young generation. But that connection with industry turned out to be unsatisfying, as the products ended up being unaffordable and expensive.

presentation of your work at the Salone del Mobile, in an alternative space from those of the Fiera (the big trade fair), was in some sense the origin of the 'Fuorisalone'? Didn't those first presentations in public spaces give rise to a phenomenon that now involves the whole city of Milan? Its whole focus for a week is on design, and hasn't this 'spilling out' from the factories to the city become the model for presenting design in many other places?

GC: That's not for me to say. But I remember that when we were finally ready, after all our cosy meetings at little lakeside restaurants, we organized the first presentation of Progetto Oggetto at the Cappellini headquarters at Carugo, in Brianza. That was in 1994. The following year we organized a spectacular presentation in Milan, at the Fabbrica del Vapore, where Jasper and James jointly created Casa Cappellini. Alongside it we organized the presentation of Progetto Oggetto, in which real objects were in

GC: It has always been the case that when we speak of design we think of industry, but we disregard the craftspeople and overlook their role in Italian design of that period. The Brianza region of those years was paradise for young designers. I recall that when I took some of them – Marc Newson, Tom Dixon, Konstantin Grcic, as well as James and Jasper – to meet the old Brianza artisans, they would go crazy. One of them was worth more than a dozen engineers. And having worked for many years with a wide variety of designers and architects, they had accumulated knowledge that was unique and original. In fact, I believe that the generational turnover is a huge problem for Italian design. Anyway, the Brianzoli have a character of their own; at first they're a little diffident, but once you understand each other they are the most generous people.

When I think back to Progetto Oggetto I realize it was a project that in its own way was Herculean from the point of view of manufacture, because we insisted on working in very diverse areas of production and with very diverse materials, some of them totally unfamiliar to us. In addition to carpentry, we went to blow Marc Newson's glass vases on Murano, we worked with an extraordinary ceramicist called Alessio Sarri, who worked for Sottsass, and we travelled round the Brescia area, where there are experts in sheet-metalworking. You couldn't do all that today. A wish to allow maximum freedom, including the use of materials, requires enormous administrative effort, even in the case of reduced numbers. In general we're used to looking at the finished product, and it's hard to communicate the complex processes involved in manufacturing an object.

FP: In a climate in which masters of Milanese design such as Achille Castiglioni and Marco Zanuso were almost unapproachable, and the Milan design scene was very clearly defined, what were the possibilities for a young firm?

GC: Acting in a very free and reckless way was certainly a key to our success. I don't deny that when I decided to develop our family business we were a very small company that made ordinary pieces of furniture and hardly knew what design was. With my youthful enthusiasm I thought I could change everything in six months, whereas now I realize that one lifetime isn't enough to do everything you want. But at that time our decision to try to understand what was happening in the world was also down to the fact that all the great Italian designers were already connected with firms with whom they had established a special, sometimes exclusive relationship. That was certainly a spur to looking for an international opening.

FP: In a way the arrival of that new generation of designers shuffled the cards again in a game we thought was over.

Zzofa for Cappellini, 1993

GC: Well, it wasn't as if there were a great many international opportunities, as there are today. And it is natural to seek out someone who is similar to yourself. At that time it was a matter of leaving a lot of room for instinct and that idea of collegiality, of relationships with others. I don't believe you can think of confining designs within rigid schemes that may be dictated by marketing departments. I always say we should do our best to let people imagine and create things that are useful, but also beautiful. Nobody needs ugly things.

Sketch for Solid, 1986

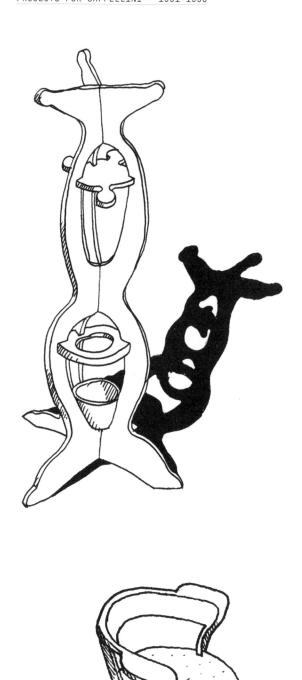

1. PICENO COLLECTION (1991)

The Piceno chair is emblematic of the series of furniture produced in beechwood by Cappellini. James designed this, his first chair, for Promosedia, the competition held annually by manufacturers in the so-called 'chair triangle', the area in the north-eastern part of the Friuli region, which at that time supplied a third of the world's wooden chairs. He won first prize.

His chair mixes its 'Modern' essence with references to the traditional idea of a chair, recognisable in the opulence of the entire series, as well as a cartoonish element, seen here in the design of the chair's feet.
- Francesca Picchi

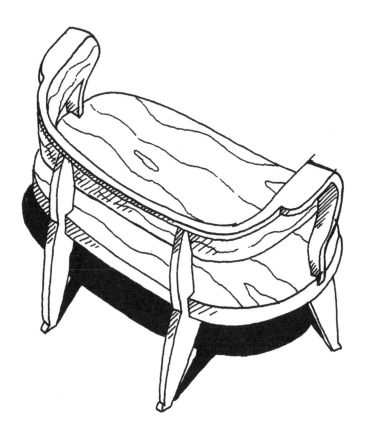

79

2. PROGETTO OGGETTO - NEW COLLECTION OF OBJECTS FOR THE HOME (1992)

The first collections of Progetto Oggetto gave total freedom to the designer as to the choice of materials for projects. This was important so as to discover and experiment in many fields of production.

The discerning customer today, is no longer just the customer who fits the stereotype of the 'well-to-do', but also the customer who is perhaps less 'well-to-do' and aware of the truth behind the products that are offered to them. The economical product is so often conceived as an imitator of a less economical product. Such outmoded concepts such as 'quantity means quality' have left so many people standing in a kitchen with peeling 'marble effect' melamine or sitting on a luxurious-looking sofa where the seat has collapsed a few years after having bought it. Today, the consumer is aware of having been taken for a ride.

The customer is in a sense coerced into forgetting the 'long term' in favour of the 'short term'. 'Wanting' rather than 'considering'. 'Resolving' rather than 'creating'. - James Irvine

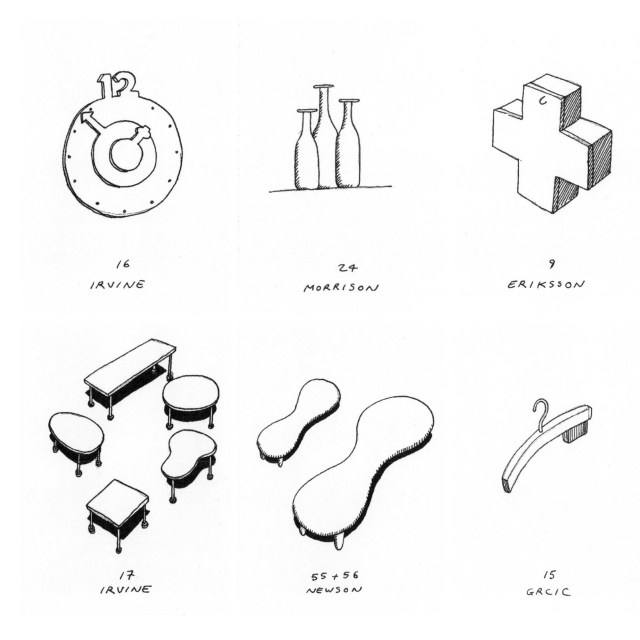

16
IRVINE

24
MORRISON

9
ERIKSSON

17
IRVINE

55 + 56
NEWSON

15
GRCIC

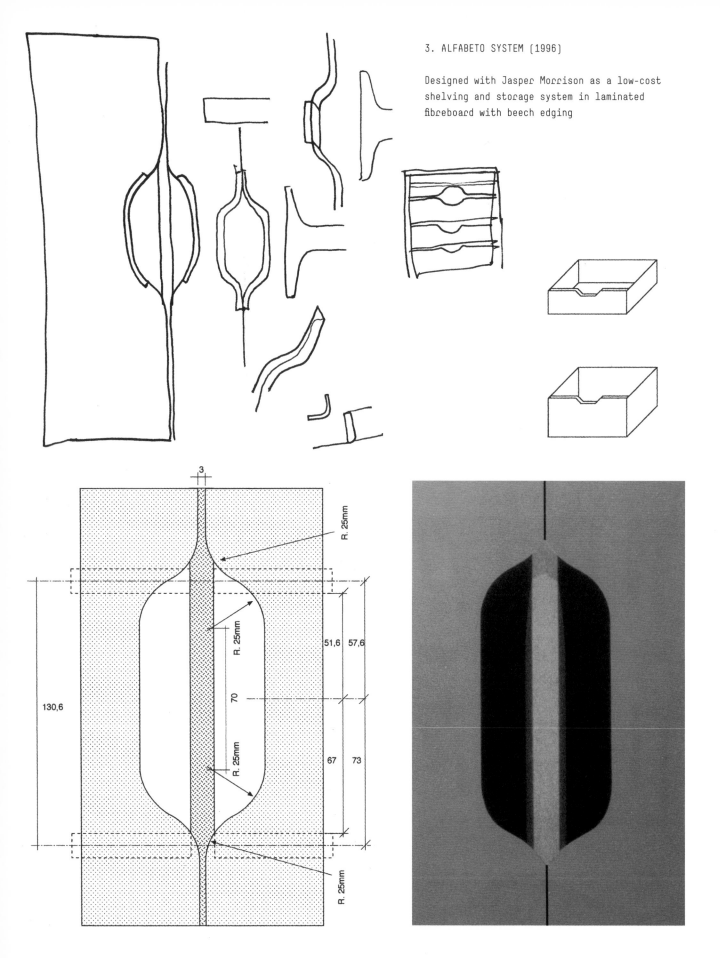

Designed with Jasper Morrison as a low-cost
shelving and storage system in laminated
fibreboard with beech edging

3

R. 25mm

R. 25mm

R. 25mm

R. 25mm

51,6 57,6

70

67 73

130,6

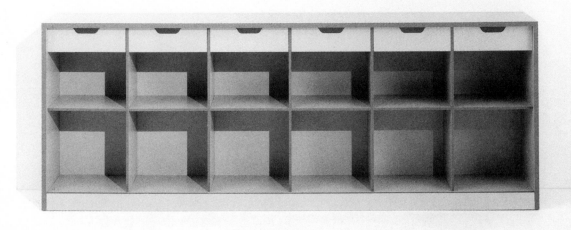

CAPPELLINI / Alfabeto System

Thomas and Anna have a small flat. They have three rooms:
a bedroom, a kitchen and a sort of living room. There
is nothing unusual about this, their place is a typical
city apartment. The bedroom has a large bed for sleeping
and romping. The room is also strewn with clothes and
shoes. It is a private place, only for them. The kitchen
is just a kitchen. There is a small table where they have
breakfast together. It's a functional space.

The living room is a kind of techno laboratory: sound
system, computer, TV and video player. It is a multifunctional space - sometimes an office, sometimes a
reading room and sometimes a place to sit with friends.
Every now and again a friend will come round and get so
drunk that they can't drive home. That's just the moment
when the sofa bed comes in handy. - James Irvine

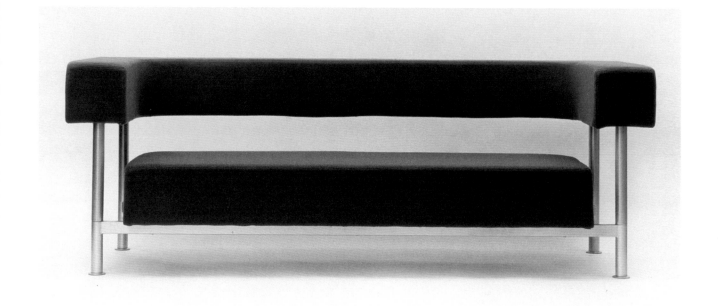

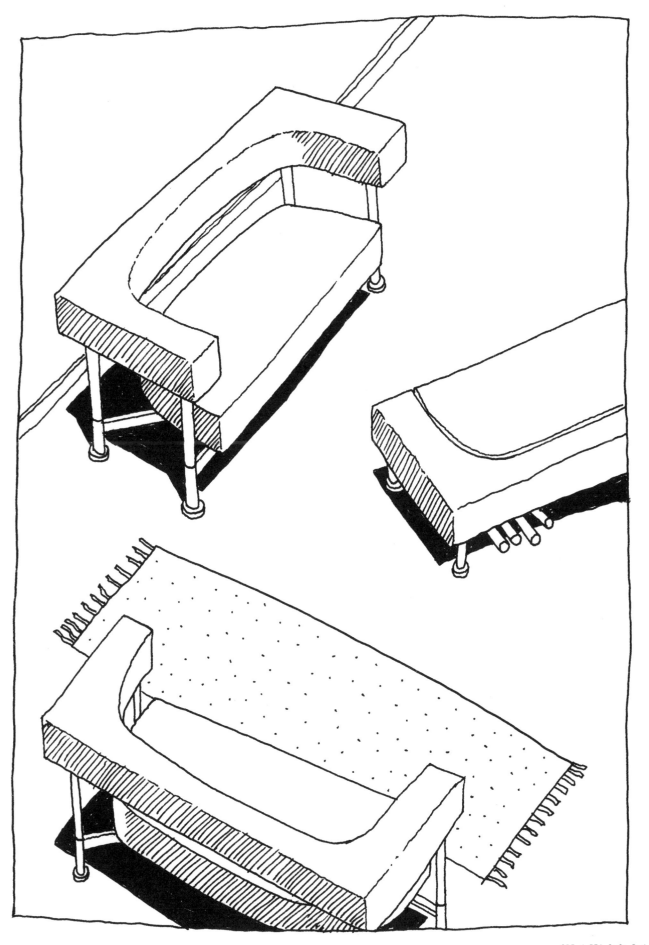

For the last fifty years Egizia have been expanding
the possibilities of a very special technique:
silk-screening on glass. The serigraphed glass used
for the products in the Handle With Care collection
acquires a dignity of its own and the quality
of the decoration is astounding. These objects
fill a home with a charge of quality and freshness
that reveals the passion of those who made them
and the enthusiasm of those who designed them.
- Marco Zanini (excerpt from catalogue)

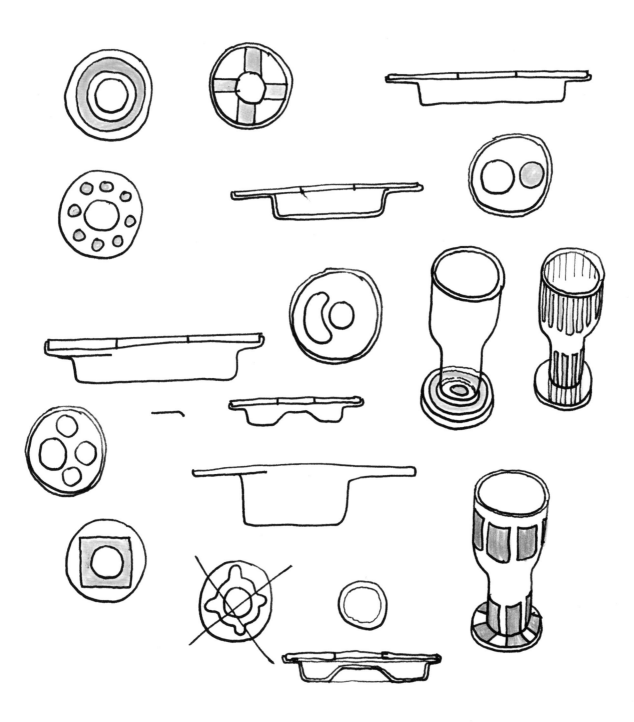

1. ARCHIVER (1994)

We launched this product with our 1994 collection at the Paul Smith showroom in Milan during the Salone. This was James's take on the classic Edwardian rotating bookcase. - Sheridan Coakley

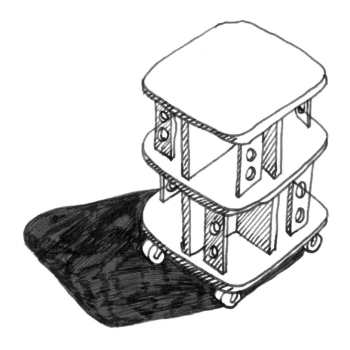

2. LOUNGE SOFA (1998)

This sofa has a traditional beech frame with foam padding and aluminium feet. At the time we didn't have our own upholstery factory - our makers struggled to get it right and unfortunately it never went into production. - Sheridan Coakley

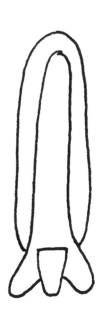

Self-assembly, free-standing shelving in lacquered MDF. This was the first product I made with James.
- Sheridan Coakley

3. EASEL MIRROR (1994)

Launched with our 1994 collection at Paul Smith alongside the Archiver, this piece was constructed from embossed lacquered MDF and mirror. This was very early use of MDF.
- Sheridan Coakley

4. HAT LAMP (1994)

Also part of the 1994 collection, this was more James's product than SCP's, in so much as he designed and had it made locally to his studio in Milan. It was never put into production.
- Sheridan Coakley

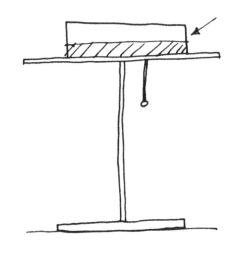

BRF was founded to collect work by young Italian
designers that have been influenced by the world
of comics. Its philosophy is to highlight the animistic
properties of objects - properties that provoke
spontaneous emotions. In this sense these pieces
of furniture present themselves as intimate companions,
as if they were not inanimate objects but friendly
pets. - Cristina Morozzi

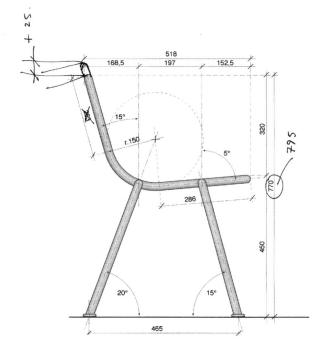

Eight people sitting round a table, discussing a product to
be tailor-made for a German client. That's how we met one evening
in 1995, at the old offices in Sant'Angelo Lodigiano of OgTM
the company specializing in making wheels for the furniture
industry that we had founded in the 1960s.

Among the designs we discussed were a wheel designed by James which
was very beautiful and innovative: there was nothing like it on
the market. Unfortunately the design for the client never took off,
but we decided to produce it by ourselves.

The deep friendship and mutual esteem between us enabled our company
to take a new direction. James also helped us to rethink our company's
image. We put our faith in a new market that hadn't previously existed
but which everyone later emulated. The mark James left on us was
unique: everyone else followed in his footsteps. The Trivini family
will never forget him. - Ruggero and Marilena Trivini

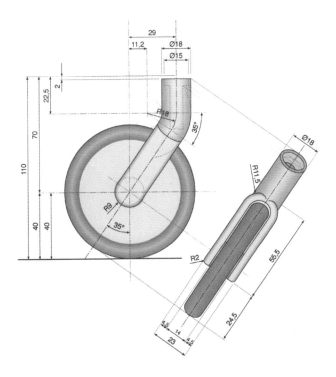

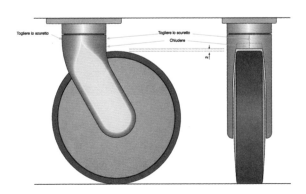

In those days, I always had lunch at a restaurant in the centre of Milan where I had established a very friendly rapport with the waiter, Luigi. Since I was so keen to design a professional bottle-opener, I asked him lots of questions about how his own opener worked. He had a big collection of different kinds - free samples from wine merchants. I thought about the project for two years, until I had designed my bottle-opener, which I immediately gift-wrapped and took to Luigi as a surprise. I was very disappointed when he turned it over in his hands and smugly dismissed it, saying it was too heavy. I felt all the arrogance of an over-confident designer that believes he can make something better... I realized that the best corkscrew is the lightest; if it breaks, it costs nothing, and in any case, it works perfectly well! - James Irvine

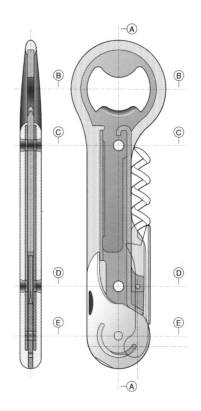

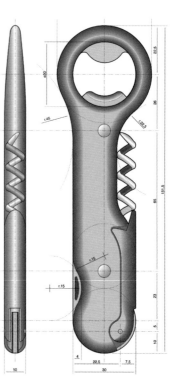

94

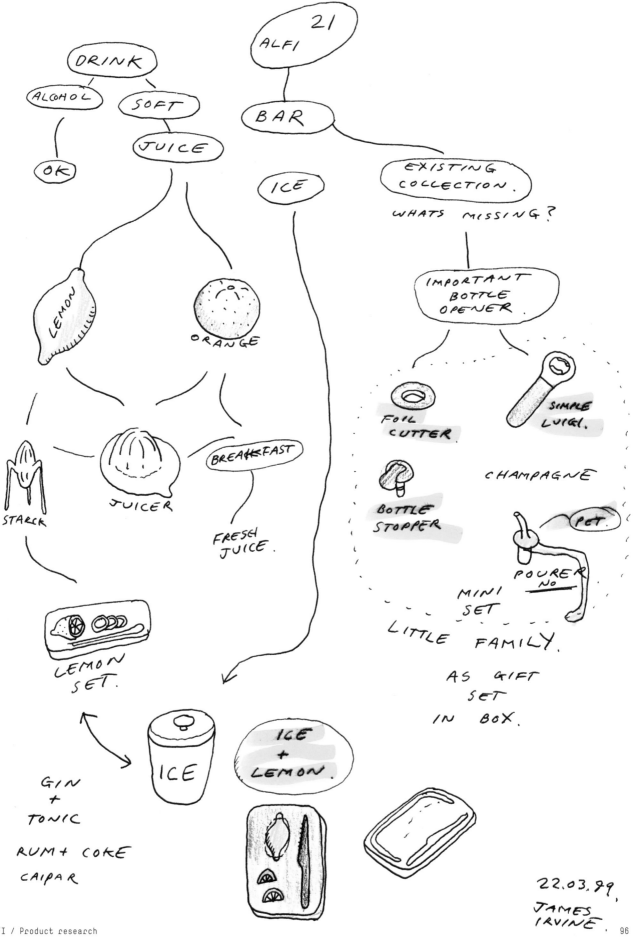

ALFI 21

DRINK
ALCOHOL
SOFT
OK
JUICE

BAR

EXISTING COLLECTION.
WHATS MISSING?

LEMON

ORANGE

ICE

IMPORTANT BOTTLE OPENER

FOIL CUTTER

SIMPLE LUIGI.

STARCK

JUICER

BREAKFAST

FRESH JUICE.

CHAMPAGNE

BOTTLE STOPPER

PET

POURER NO

MINI SET

LITTLE FAMILY.

AS GIFT SET IN BOX.

LEMON SET.

ICE

ICE + LEMON.

GIN + TONIC
RUM + COKE
CAIPAR

22.03.99.
JAMES IRVINE.

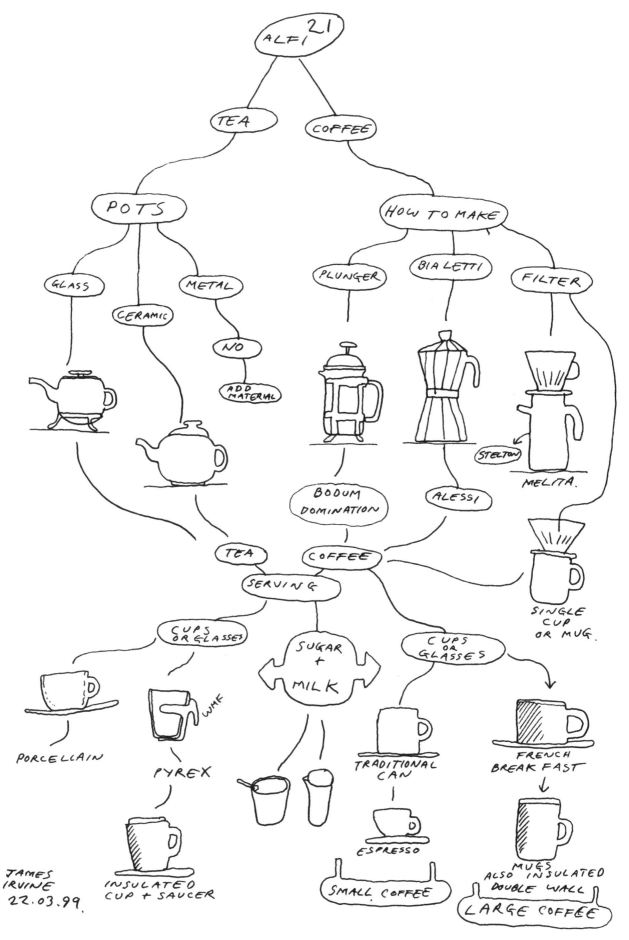

ALFI 21

TEA — COFFEE

POTS

GLASS
CERAMIC
METAL
NO
ADD MATERIAL

HOW TO MAKE

PLUNGER
BIALETTI
FILTER

STELTON

MELITA.

BODUM DOMINATION
ALESSI

SINGLE CUP OR MUG.

TEA — COFFEE

SERVING

CUPS OR GLASSES

SUGAR + MILK

CUPS OR GLASSES

PORCELLAIN

PYREX

WMF

INSULATED CUP + SAUCER

TRADITIONAL CAN

ESPRESSO

SMALL COFFEE

FRENCH BREAKFAST

MUGS ALSO INSULATED DOUBLE WALL

LARGE COFFEE

JAMES IRVINE 22.03.99.

This rug is typical of what James ironically called
his 'sausage period', for the use of the sausage-like
shape found in many of his designs from this time.
- Francesca Picchi

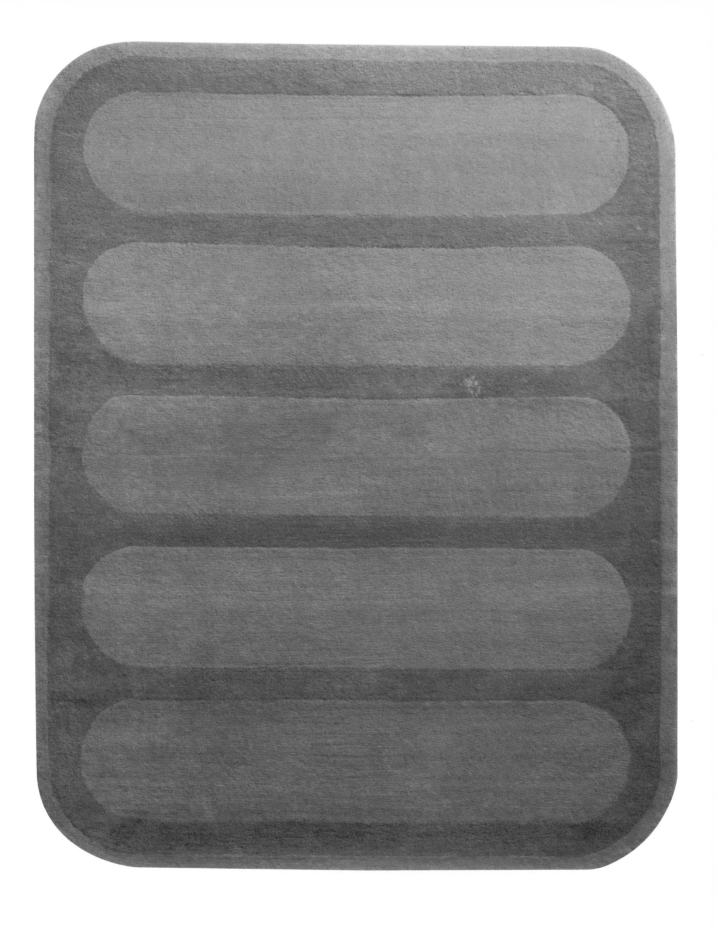

1. FLIK COLLECTION (1998)

This was one the first designs created using
gas-injection moulding, which we used to produce
the chair's seat and back, before mounting them
on to a metal frame. Aiming to keep costs to a
minimum, James designed a single element that
could be replicated in the same way for both the
seat and the back: an organically-shaped 'slat'.
This element ultimately made the overall design
of the chair totally coherent. - Eugenio Perazza

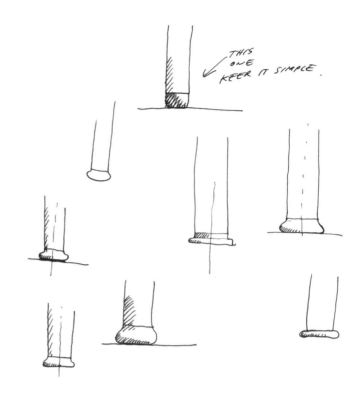

2. CENTOMILA COLLECTION (1999)

The name Centomila ('one hundred thousand') came before the chair itself - inspired by both its retail price and also its predicted annual sales: 100,000 units at the basic price of 100,000 lire. We developed the idea for this project with a design classic - the tubular steel chair - in mind.

James's design of the chair retained its minimalist form and enhanced it with a distinctive detail: the flattening of the steel tube where the ring supporting the seat meets the vertical line of the leg. Thus he was able to transform a problem into a distinguishing trait: a gesture that turns the most critical part of the structure into something beautiful.
- Eugenio Perazza

1. LUNAR (1998)

During the early years of his career, James received quite a number of commissions for sofa beds, to the extent that he became known almost as a specialist in their design. Although new inventions were constantly being brought out, James never showed great interest in the mechanics of the sofa bed, but instead concentrated on the ease of the movements required to trigger the change of use, whilst preserving an overall conceptual simplicity. The name of this sofa, and the design of its feet are clear allusions to man's epic landing on the moon, which James had witnessed as a child.
- Francesca Picchi

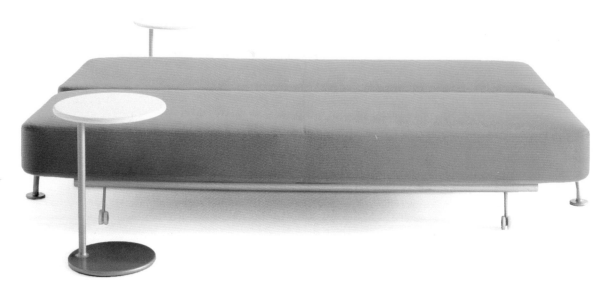

2. POLAR (1999)

One-off piece realized for an exhibition
curated by *Wallpaper** magazine.

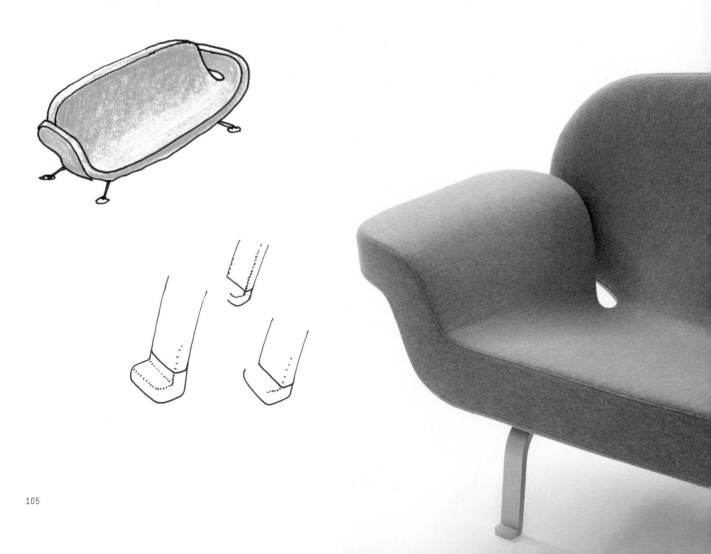

3. RADAR (2001)

Read a book, watch TV, sip on a gin
and tonic, take a quick nap, play
Space Invaders on your portable
laptop computer, eat peanuts, spin
around, sign an important contract
for millions of dollars, chat on the
phone, read the paper, contemplate
your future, contemplate your past.
Take it easy, relaxing in Radar.
- James Irvine

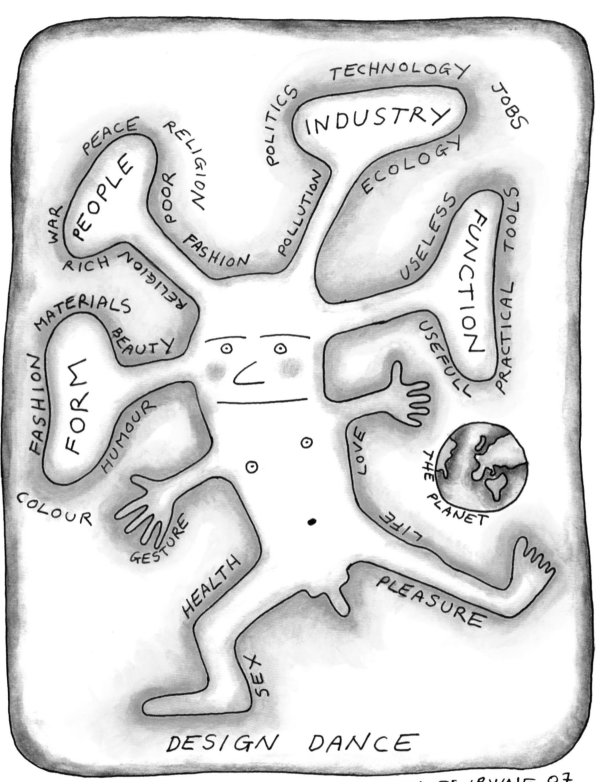

STEFANO GIOVANNONI

SCULPTURES OF THE INDUSTRIAL AGE

Table lighters, Hong Kong project, Design Gallery Milano, 1992

FRANCESCA PICCHI: You and James represent a new generation that emerged in the same years and the same context: 1980s post-Memphis Milan. You were close friends, but you had very different approaches to design. Could it be said that you had parallel histories but often took opposite directions? Which aspects of your approaches to design brought you together and which divided you?

STEFANO GIOVANNONI: It all went back to our training, which was very different. James trained at the Royal College of Art, London, where there was a pragmatic culture that tended to see the design course as evolving on the basis of established archetypes. I always started from a concept: my post-Radical training gave me a hostile attitude towards professional design, and I wanted to reclaim the culture of commercial products, in contrast to traditional design culture. In a different way, James was also critical of the wilder excesses of our profession and thought our work had an educational and ethical mission. I questioned the positive practice of industrial design, but at the same time I defended any product that was commercially successful, in so far as I believed it responded to a cultural expression of the social context.

James was intolerant of the fanciful impulse of designers to go overboard on the intrinsic reality of an object. He was very critical of the way objects were loaded with a language too remote from their real essence. If I was designing a salt and pepper set, I would see it as a personality with very different characteristics from those we were used to, starting from the materials. James, on the other hand, would tackle it according to his experiences and memory.

FP: You met in Milan in the period immediately following Memphis. It could be said that one of the priorities for your generation of designers was to rebuild your relationship with industry, which was heavily questioned during the years of Radical research. I think your different aproaches can be illustrated by two episodes that have little in common but that throw a clear light on those years. The first was Progetto Oggetto, for Cappellini and the second was Alessi's project Family Follows Fiction, launched in 1993. How do you see them today?

SG: From the late 1980s onwards, after years of experimentation with different idioms, there was clearly a rapprochement with industry. In those years Cappellini was trying to establish itself as a magnet for young designers with an international perspective. It was determined to bring new energies to the world of Milanese design, which was dominated by the presence of the big names. Progetto Oggetto therefore placed itself within that research context.

Alessi's Family Follows Fiction was the most radical campaign conducted within a company with its own established culture. In contrast to Cappellini, who worked in a semi-artisanal context, Alessi had an industrial tradition behind it, based on steel technology. The project devised for Alessi chose to use plastic, a material very different from steel, which was the company's core business and involved greater quantities and investments. Plastic revolutionized the very nature of the company, which had started out by making products in short runs, driving it towards more up-to-date approaches to products and marketing, while Progetto Oggetto marked a return to craftsmanship. Its financial impact was very different.

Following that operation, Alessi saw its sales triple, above all because it focused on a new and completely different market, and succeeded in getting its message across to a younger public. Both, however, were experiments involving youth culture and the way young people viewed industrially-produced goods from very different points of view. They certainly offered James and me many opportunities for discussion.

FP: The figure of Ettore Sottsass dominated the Milanese design scene in the 1980s. James was Sottsass's business partner, and you worked in his studio, but you chose to pursue different idioms. How do you interpret your relationship with him?

SG: James always remained independent. I also worked in Sottsass's studio but I never conformed to his style. So I understand how people worked in the studio, and their relationship with Ettore. For that reason I think I can see James's hand in many of the designs produced by Sottsass Associati. There are certain features, certain solutions, that aren't typical of Sottsass's idiom, but are in fact the fruit of James's way of thinking. For example, if we take an object like the Cloud Chair, which Sottsass Associati designed for ICF, you can see James's hand, even in the design of the sections. Ettore never designed that kind of radial feature: he would have designed a round or square section, something related to primary geometry, anyway. I recall that when I was working in his studio I designed a section that was rounded off, and while he accepted that detail, he discussed it at length, because it was a discordant element in his idiom.

FP: In the debate over design in the 1980s there were some distinct polarities: modernism and post-modernism, minimalism and Memphis, Gute Form and Pop aesthetics. Where does James's work fit in that context?

SG: Although he never identified himself with minimalism, James always showed an impulse to search for what was essential. I think one of his greatest virtues was to have introduced a new degree of freedom and a touch of Pop into the minimalist idiom whose conceptual basis he basically shared. This 'Pop' mentality in his work was that playful, ironic element that helped him find his own idiom, disrupting the inherent rigour of his British training. That ironic turn was the most genuine expression of his character. He liked to give a final twist of humour or surprise, giving the object completely new characteristics.

Nevertheless, the 1980s were characterized by the search for a personal idiom. To have one's own recognizable style was fundamental; otherwise you didn't exist. Anything was acceptable as long as it was distinctive. It was a very different logic from that of mass-produced industrial design, which tends to stick to the familiar. We were looking for what was new, and new meant turning your back on what had existed before. James was following a different path, a double one, if you like, because he had first worked for Olivetti and then for Sottsass Associati and at the same time he was immersed in all the issues arising at his own studio.

Cloud Chair for ICF designed by Sottsass Associati, 1998

FP: Did you often discuss your work?

SG: I recall an evening when James, Jasper Morrison and I were sitting at the dinner table and we got lost in a long discussion about two of my designs. I had just designed the Bombo Stool for Magis, and even if they were perhaps not totally sympathetic to the design, they thought it was a much more important project than the Girotondo I had designed for Alessi. But it was the exact opposite for me: I thought the Girotondo was the design of my life, from which everything else flowed.

I didn't fully understand the position James and Jasper took regarding my work. I didn't understand why they loved some of my designs but couldn't feel positive about others. In some respects I would have thought the Girotondo, which is a minimal, conceptual design, was in keeping with the way James and Jasper thought, but then I realized that the human figure was something entirely alien to their thinking. For me it represented the idea of the 'found', rather than the 'designed' object, while the iconic, stylized little man, and the figurative language, suggested an object of memory to me, putting it in the domain of popular culture. But for them an object had to spring from its archetypal essence, even if it was close to popular culture, but made contemporary through the design process. Mine was a communicative gesture. I refused to design an object while at the same time distancing myself from professional practice.

STEFANO GIOVANNONI

FP: At a time dominated by a passion for design, everything was 'designed', and loaded with expression; to declare that design was not so necessary was a rather eccentric, even strident choice, given the prevailing mood. Where did that rejection come from?

SG: We had studied for years with Remo Buti, who was a purist. During that time he had distanced himself from minimalism and was fascinated by the creativity that was rooted in popular culture. As his students, over the ten years during which we worked in Florence, Guido Venturini and I became interested in introducing dissonant elements into concepts of design, contaminating it with kitsch and making it more entertaining and expressive. I remember that among the places Guido loved to go were the station newsstands, where we would stop and look at things like snow globes or 3D postcards in which Christ opened and closed his eyes.

James and Jasper, on the other hand, represented a completely opposite approach. If they had to design a chair they would choose the ten models they considered most important in the history of chair-making, and then meld them together in a new way, pared down and brought up to date. I was interested in starting with the object so that I could make it the focus of communication. James and Jasper didn't endorse that approach. There was much in their way of seeing that I didn't understand.

For example, why James and Jasper liked the Merdolino toilet brush set so much (James had bought several for his home and office) and yet were very critical about other designs of mine. I couldn't understand why they thought the Lilliput salt and pepper set was a pointless object but the Merdolino made sense to them. Perhaps because the Merdolino was an object whose origin was the vase, itself an object of memory, and the seedling was a 'designed' object, while the salt and pepper belonged to the idiom of the comic strip and broke completely with any reference to the past.

FP: Despite James's close relationship with Jasper, I'd like you to help us understand the differences in their professional approches.

SG: James had a very distinct identity of his own. Of course, he and Jasper shared a common background derived from their type of professional training – the 'Anglo-Saxon' school – but on coming into contact with the Milan scene, James merged the two worlds. That's an achievement that should be acknowledged. James managed to introduce into design a degree of freedom in contrast with the minimalism that was in danger of becoming a sterile language if applied too rigidly. Minimalism was the expression of a culture that tended to exclude and deny diversity, in contrast with the need felt by contemporary culture, in which James was deeply immersed, to be welcoming, inclusive and mixed – features that were also part of his character.

From his first designs James showed he was trying to find objects that were sensuous and full of feeling, which were entirely alien to minimalism. And despite his rigorous thinking, Jasper too had fun indulging in gestures which are impossible to relate to a strictly minimalist spirit, as we see, for example, in the wavy design of one of his first sofas for Cappellini. If I had to identify a common logic in their approach I would definitely say it was a search for form via memory, or at least via a language that was faithful to the object. There's a touch of Pop in James's work. He has always expressed that element very strongly: he enjoyed designing and wanted every object to have an element of fun. James put a considerable amount of play, albeit controlled, into a design. He was fascinated by tradition but at the same time he immediately wanted to question it.

FP: James always did a lot of drawings, especially throughout the 1980s and 1990s, before we used computers. In the Irvine archives there's a whole series of experimental works from that period that show great freedom, even in their references. What do you recognize in his drawing style?

SG: James worked through asymmetry and the way the parts of the object exist in a state of controlled tension. That way of splitting up the object, dismantling it, playing with asymmetry and putting

Pink Punk Fitzsu Grand Prix toy car for Playsam, 2006

its parts out of alignment, belongs to Sottsass's compositional approach, and in James it was tempered by his British education and upbringing. I recall that when he arrived from England he drew in a very different way: being in Milan was a big influence.

What I saw at once in James that was different from me, was that way of breaking up the object in order to create dynamics among the parts, something I tended not to do, since I adhered to a way of designing that rejected the compositional approach. I have always been interested in different dynamics, analogy, for example; I rejected point blank the search for composition and all the practices connected with the design of the object, in favour of analogy.

For James, on the other hand, asymmetry was a way of disturbing the equilibrium of the object and determining the internal dynamics from which the design emerged. In his designs you can always see a small transgression, a slight anomaly which became his hallmark: he often showed me it, laughing as he did so. Let's say James worked with composition and language (as did Sottsass), while I tried to bypass them. Something important that James learned from Sottsass was the idea of colour. Sottsass had such a strong sense of colour that he would ask you, 'Draw me a red house or a green vase.' What he meant, was that the colour was in the object's DNA.

FP: But that was also a period in which everyone enjoyed sketching and drawing.

SG: Let's say there was a lot to discover. In fact, here was a feeling that everything was still to be discovered. Memphis and Alchimia had revolutionized the world of design, and so we had glimpsed the existence of a whole new world to be explored, outside the thinking of Vico Magistretti or Marco Zanuso. There was so much energy in the air. We started projects without knowing where we would end up. It was also a way of starting out as a designer. You only have to think of Ron Arad's Concrete Stereo. Those objects served as reference points in defining a language with which to identify yourself.

The 1980s were a time of searching for a language, of tremendous energy and possibilities. Every designer, like an artist, had to invent one of their own in order to be recognized. We young designers judged our work by its distinctiveness.

With the King-Kong project we were working with unusual, innovative materials like silicones, metalized

Sketches for Emaux des Récollets Longwy vases

polyurethanes and crumpled metals, looking for things that were impossible, and remote from commercial considerations. Looking again at James's sketches, you can see that tension in the search for a language of his own. With their great rigour, they form an important and highly original part of his work.

FP: Is it true that the dinner table was your favourite place for discussing design?

SG: We often had dinner together. James liked traditional places with an authentic local flavour. He loved the sense of human contact, restaurants where the owner tries to get to know his customers, and as James was very friendly he knew how to form solid relationships with people. I could list the places that marked the various periods of our friendship, the Bar Basso being the first.

For restaurants, there was the long period of Il Rigolo, then one serving dishes from the Abruzzo, Neve e Fuoco. He loved the fact that those were the actual names of the people who ran it. Then, of course, La Torre di Pisa, where Sottsass was a regular. The food often took second place to the atmosphere, and as I was becoming a serious gourmet I sometimes didn't approve of his choices. I was happy to go to places with character, but I wanted to eat well. And more recently he liked Chinese restaurants. But the Bar Basso was always our favourite. James found it when he had his studio nearby and he took everyone there.

He made friends rights away with Maurizio (the son of the founder, who had been Arrigo Cipriani's partner at Harry's Bar, in Venice) and it soon became our regular meeting place. One year, James suggested holding a party at the Bar Basso. It involved him and four friends: Jasper, Marc Newson, Peter Allen and me. Each of us bought thirty vouchers for the drinks and that way we funded the first party, which was a great success, because the whole Milan design world came, as well as all the foreign visitors to the Salone del

STEFANO GIOVANNONI

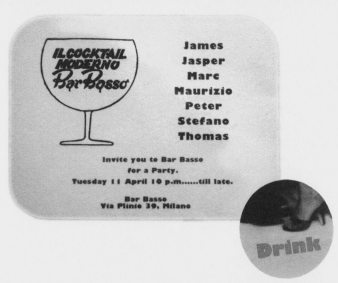

Invitation and drinks token for the inaugural Bar Basso party, 1999

Mobile. It immediately became a ritual. That success gave us the idea of creating a group we called Big Snake, in which Jasper, Marc, Peter, James and I tried to get some design projects going as a group.

One year, after the Salone del Mobile, we went to Capri, where we had been invited to discuss design and sex, a rather odd subject around which to construct an actual project. Every discussion, every sigh, was being recorded, from when we got up in the morning, until evening. But that was it.

FP: How do you think his language changed over the years?

SG: James was always the complete professional. Unlike many other designers he avoided concentrating exclusively on furniture: he was very interested in technical objects, partly, for example, thanks to his relationship with Olivetti. The key thing was the great pleasure James took in designing, building the prototype, and seeing the object emerge and take shape.

When I went to his studio I found innumerable little models in cardboard and wood, because the objects had to be made by hand. He was so good at making prototypes. He would start from the two-dimensional drawing, and took pleasure in turning the shapes into three-dimensional objects. Many designers seem to find creativity rather painful, but he enjoyed it and communicated that feeling to those around him, as if he took special joy in involving others in the game of creation.

FP: Do you see a change in his repertoire of formal references in more recent years?

SG: Perhaps the change had more to do with the companies with whom he was working. Let's put it like this, James was an industrial designer who suffered from the decline in Italy's technological industries. He suffered from the fact that Olivetti and many similar firms reached the end of the road at the time we were designing. Although we were both industrial designers, we managed to work with small or medium-sized companies, often using semi-artisanal, rather than truly industrial methods. Over time, Italian design became increasingly associated with furniture, and that was certainly a negative factor for our generation. But although James had designed beautiful industrial products like his printers for Olivetti, and technical ones for Toshiba and Whirlpool, he was also attracted to the domestic, familiar, intimate and personal aspects of small and medium-sized firms in Italy.

FP: Your generation had to deal with the question of consumer goods in a world that was becoming ever more mediatized and was expressing a need for objects that spoke a language everyone could understand. In those years there was a lot of talk about 'ludic' objects, specifically about yours – what do you think?

SG: When Alessi spoke of a 'toy object', I was furious. I was interested in the consumer side of things. I hadn't the least interest in talking about the ludic. I started from the presumption that the object was seen as a status symbol and functioned as an indicator of social status. I've always tried to take the drama out of that relationship between man and object, and to make objects that would do more, in that they were in empathy with the person who bought them. Objects that would be in direct contact with us but not as obstacles between us and others.

I designed objects with an identity, characters with a soul, which would be in harmony with us instead of being vehicles that represent us. I never thought about Disney when I was designing my products. My basic idea came from Jean Baudrillard, from reading his *System of Objects* (1968), based on his thoughts about a society that was becoming ever more mediatized, pervaded by consumerism. Given that communication and the market have always been central for me, I was interested in the world of media and I therefore thought of objects in terms of communication. If an object doesn't communicate, it doesn't sell. It's like a TV programme without an audience – you turn it off. That's why I've always tried to see the essence of the industrial product in communication with the public at large.

The world had changed compared with that of people like Vico Magistretti, Achille Castiglioni and Marco Zanuso; there was a need for objects with a different mediatic power from that of traditional design, which in any case was always a niche culture. Design has never had mediatic power, but these objects marked a change of pace and anticipated what happened later.

FP: The world of consumerism and the market compelled design to leave the niche in which it was enclosed. In that respect, another thing that brings you together from different positions is your relationship with popular culture. What was your attitude towards it?

SG: James was drawn to popular culture, at all levels and in all areas of everyday life – from the fact that he liked a certain kind of restaurant, trattoria or hotel, to a certain kind of anonymous traditional object. Above all, he was drawn to objects that had a strong cultural history, created by generations of nameless craftsmen. That interest emerged in the smallest details, of every sort, from deciding which restaurant to go to, to planning a holiday or where to play the game of bocce. Even his passion for bocce indicates his interest in a certain type of popular culture.

Once, Jasper and James infected all the rest of the group with that passion, to the point of organizing proper bocce tournaments. They all took part: Marc Newson, Peter Allen and Fabrice Domercq. I was less keen, because for me bocce belongs to a different world: it makes me think of old-age pensioners. But I think that episode illustrates the attraction to a type of culture I could only define as popular, in which James and Jasper both had a great interest.

And James, as an Englishman, was fascinated by a certain type of traditional Italian culture: the one that had led him to settle in Milan and to love Italy with a passion that at times I couldn't understand. It was probably that popular world, more traditional and deeply embedded, that attracted him. As for the differences between us, let's say I was interested in

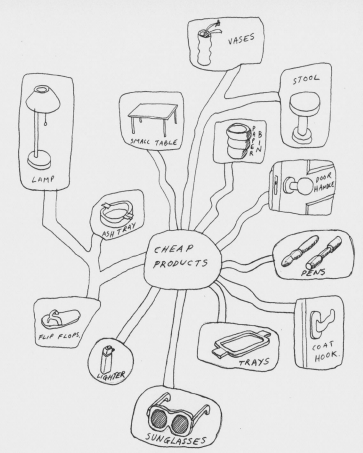

Sketch for Popular Cheap Products project, early 1990s

the exaggerated, surreal, kitsch aspects of popular culture and its imagination.

James and Jasper, on the other hand, looked at popular culture from an educated perspective. They saw its phenomena as part of a context, as tools that could describe a culture of belonging. I think that also explains their passion for the worlds of bocce and wine, for a relationship with material things based on actual need. I believe they saw mass-produced goods as having contaminated the purity of the object and, compared with the original, having vulgarized it and the meanings it expressed, which they tried to recover by a process of 'excavation'. I believe the world of consumption is a necessity for industrial society. So for me, mass production did not contaminate objects, but by differentiating them extended the market and fostered a multiplicity of languages and alternatives more in keeping with a multicultural society.

We occupied very different positions, but it's also true that our generation was the first to be swept along on the tide of consumerism and the arrival of computers, the internet and globalization. Everything changed so fast, and as a consequence our work and our strategies also had to change.

STEFANO GIOVANNONI

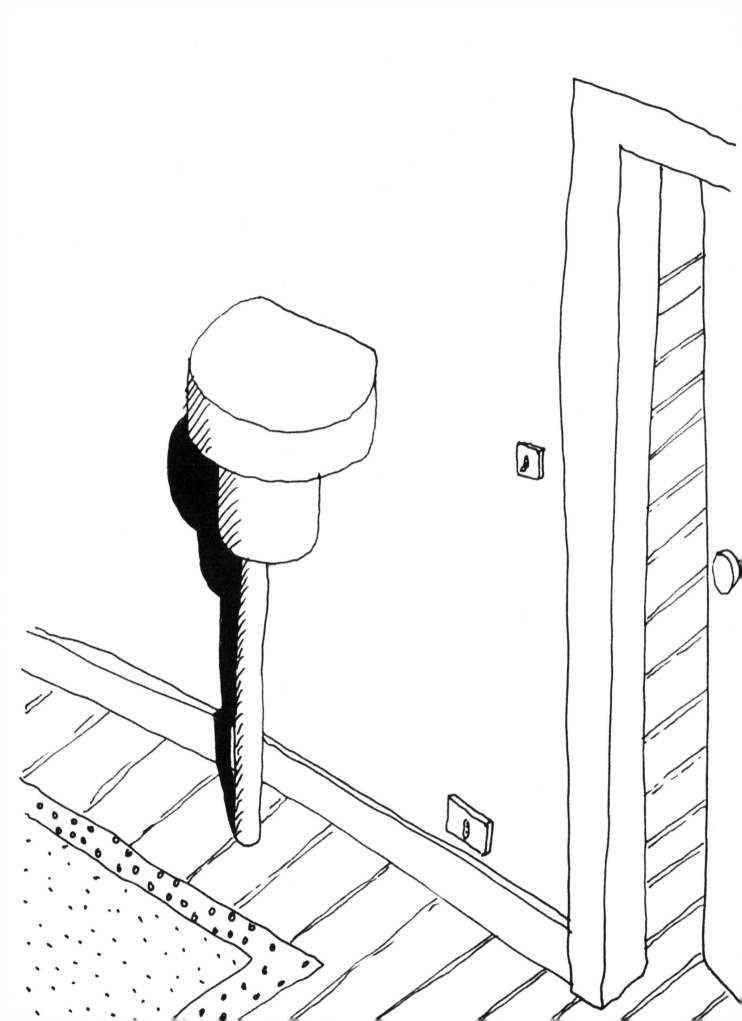

KONSTANTIN GRCIC

PLAYFULNESS
IN THE
ORDINARY RITUALS
OF
FUNCTIONALITY

James Irvine's studio in Viale Piceno, late 1990s

FRANCESCA PICCHI: You and James were united by a deep friendship and shared design projects over many years. What were your aspirations as designers?

KONSTANTIN GRCIC: I first met James in September 1988 while I was in Milan for the Salone del Mobile. I stayed in a small hotel on Viale Piceno. One morning, as I was standing outside my hotel, I saw Jasper Morrison and James come out from the courtyard next door, which happened to be James's home and studio. I remember visiting that studio on Viale Piceno on several occasions after this first encounter. The office was in a four-room apartment across from the flat where he lived. The building was probably from the 1930s – it had a lot of daylight and high ceilings. At the time there were no computers of course, just a fax machine, a telephone, and drawing boards. The different rooms, all diverting off a long corridor, were sparsely furnished: tables and chairs, some prototypes, some vintage pieces James had collected. As far as I remember, Jasper was renting one of the rooms as his Milan base.

James was still working as a partner at Sottsass Associati, but starting to run his own independent studio simultaneously. That was the big dream for our generation – to have our own studio and to work for industry. The most accessible model was that of the Italian family-run companies, like the Brianza based furniture manufacturers. Most of us started our professional careers this way, working for small design driven manufacturers in northern Italy. Milan was definitively the gate for entering into this world.

FP: Over time, however, the freedom to make and experiment, which was represented by small manufacturers, has become a limitation.

KG: I remember that during those years, in the early 1990s, there was a clear shortlist of companies one would have wanted to work with. Cappellini was one of them, as was Driade, Alias and some others. These companies marked a perspective for us young designers, which felt good. It felt like the right thing to do. I guess that everyone made their own experiences during their first years in business, good and bad. It was quite easy to get into the system and to get first things produced by these companies. However, over time, we started to question things. What we poured into our work didn't match what we got back. We all had to realize how small and limited the industry was that we were working for.

I am still hanging in there, because there is a lot I love about it. But, I understand that today's young designers have lost interest in following our path. Working for these small and middle-sized companies has lost its attraction simply because it seems slow and limiting. Instead, there are other, more dynamic and more autonomous ways for the young designers to build their careers. The internet has changed everything. It creates the illusion that you no longer need industry as a partner. It seems possible to succeed on one's own, not only managing a design office but also a business, producing and distributing by yourself. All alone.

Even though I can see the possibilities in this new way of doing things, it's disappointing to see a whole generation turn its back on something that still has great potential: I still believe in the world of manufacturers and specialists. There are fantastic companies and extraordinary people within these companies with the skills, know-how and experience to bring huge prospects to every new design project. Working with a 3D printer means missing out on a precious momentum, the constructive dialogue which can feed huge extra potential into any project. If we think about it, without this close relationship between designers and manufacturers some of the great masterpieces of design wouldn't have existed.

I remember in the early days, James and I were both working for a small Scandinavian company called CBI. I happened to be in Milan one day and we met for drinks in the evening. James told me about a project he had sent to Stockholm that day. He was so excited by this event – the sensation of sending a drawing through the fax machine and then, within an hour or so, receiving a call from CBI about how much they liked his design and that they wanted to produce it.

I tell this story because it illustrates how beautifully simple it was to do projects in those days. The scale of everything was so much smaller, more immediate and personal. There was always a commercial side to the work, but it was never the driving force. Our collaborations with companies were built on very personal relationships and on the feeling that we were in it for a shared passion. You gave and received on equal terms. I don't think this is just a romantic view of industry, but rather a belief in the possibilities of such collaboration. It's through this kind of critical dialogue that an idea can grow to its full potential. A feeling of community is what I associate with our generation, and James impersonated this in a very special, very particular way.

FP: This idea of design as a collaborative process is something that is apparent throughout James's career: it was an essential part of the Cappellini project in the early 1990s, but it is also present in his later works for Marsotto and Muji. Do you think that his vision about design and experimentation as something to cultivate in a group could be seen as a legacy of his experiences working with Sottsass?

KG: Yes, it was the same kind of model. He created a community of friends, sharing and building something together. It was never an exclusive club of people doing things for ourselves – it was much bigger than that.

FP: In a sense, your generation, taking industry as a kind of measure for reality, had to rebuild the relationship with industrial manufacture, which had been broken during the Radical years.

The Magis showroom, Milan, 2012 (L-R: James Irvine, Konstantin Grcic and Eugenio Perazza, founder of Magis)

KG: Exactly. The previous generation had broken that relationship and we were the ones to rebuild it. We believed that design was about the product: that something has to be produced, distributed, and ultimately, function. Industry provided the 'reality check' for our ideas.

FP: Do you see a link between the experiments that James took part in during the late 1980s and his subsequent work?

KG: When I first met James, he was working on the Solid project with the group of designers around Michele De Lucchi's studio. In my view, Solid had a very formalistic approach, but James had an interest in the ordinary rituals of functionality in things. He was creating his own language for it. Progetto Oggetto, the project James, Jasper and Giulio Cappellini created together, had a similar approach: the project was about quotidian things, about re-visiting the nature of those every day objects that surrounded us.

FP: This was probably the first time that different people from the most disparate parts of the world were perceived as a new generation of designers: in a sense you were the first globalized generation. And despite your strong individual personalities, in the end you were perceived as a group. Can you define the connection that united you?

KG: Our generation came just after movements like Memphis had opened things up. They had liberated design from certain academic doctrines and professional preconceptions. One could say that they had prepared the stage for us. The transition from the 1980s to the 1990s was more of a logical next step from the events of the 1980s. We were focused on working with companies and creating real products, not just prototypes or concepts. I think that was what we all believed in, but we were not really a group, we just happened to all be there at the same time, sharing a certain spirit, an approach, even an urgency. That's what made us a generation.

I never really thought of us as 'the first globalized generation', as you put it. Memphis was already quite international, including designers from France, England, Italy, Japan. It is true however, that in the early 1990s there were a lot of young designers from different countries starting to work for the various Italian companies on the scene. I was in Germany, others in the Netherlands, Britain or Sweden, and so on. Giulio Cappellini certainly played a significant role in this. Cappellini was the first Italian company to work with Jasper Morrison, Marc Newson, Tom Dixon and many others. For a lot of us he created the opportunity of having our first projects realized in Italy and that very often laid the crucial foundation for later careers.

FP: What part do you think James played in that connection?

KG: James was an important connecting point for all of us. For any of us foreigners, James was the link with Milan, with the Italian furniture industry, but also with its lifestyle. James was truly British, but he had adopted the Milanese way of life and he brought it to us. Taking us to his favourite restaurants and bars was a real treat. I think that everyone who knew James had their own personal connection with him. Whoever went to Milan called James, passed by his studio or met him for a drink. James was always welcoming, he was

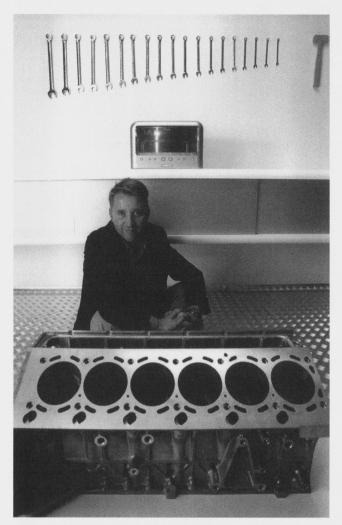

Irvine at the Whirlpool exhibition of conceptual studies for a microwave oven, 2001

the turnstile of design traffic coming into Milan – I started coming to Milan in the early 1990s, and even ten, fifteen years later, the younger designers still ended up connecting with James.

FP: From the point of view of design, what was it that you and James had in common and what made you feel different from him?

KG: We shared a lot of interests, not only in design, but also other things such as music, cars and bikes. James was older than me and that made him feel like a big brother. I learnt a lot from him and I could always go to him for advice. His experience of working with Sottsass certainly had a great influence on him, on his approach to design. It was a very humanistic approach, one that put people at the centre of everything. James definitively believed that design could help make this world a better place. But he was

Progetto Oggetto logo, 1992

not a designer that wanted to change the world. In fact, he had a very strong belief in preserving a certain form of object or ritual. We didn't always agree. Sometimes I felt a stronger need to be more radical – I was ready to turn things upside down. Why do things have to be the way they are? Can't they be different? We had a lot of interesting discussions about this.

Over the years, James and I worked for a lot of the same companies and sometimes even on the same projects, like the one for Whirlpool. Whirlpool had invited both of us (and a group of other designers) to develop future concepts for the microwave oven. The project was totally outside the reality of my normal work and I was so happy to have James around, as a friend I could turn to for advice. My instinctive (and rather naive) approach was to change everything, which meant re-inventing the product from ground up – how it worked, how it looked. James, on the other hand, kept quite closely to what microwave ovens usually are. He didn't question the 'box', and how it worked. He simply changed the way of interacting with it. He designed a beautiful sliding door that opened vertically, rather than the normal hinged doors which need a lot of space for opening. He even built a radio into it, because he felt that this would give the product yet another dimension of use. Cooking, and eating and listening to the radio. It was a beautiful idea, so simple, charming.

The project says a lot about James, about his design thinking, about his view on the world. I learnt a lot from that. I envied his way of looking at things, of really understanding the object, and accepting it for what it was. Ironically, his project really changed the microwave, while mine simply looked different. My project, trying to be radical, in the end wasn't radical at all. Mine was a formal exercise, his was more sincere. James had looked at the object very carefully, accepting its reality and working on the details, refinements and also, the user's relationship with it.

Another time we worked on parallel projects, I was designing a new pen for Lamy and James was working on one for A.G. Spalding & Bros. James did his in a year, mine took almost four years, during which we tried to rethink the pen's mechanical parts. I remember him laughing at me, asking me how I could be so naive to believe that the world needed a pen that worked differently from the way pens work. His pen was much like his microwave design, accepting how things are and looking at the details, the overall quality and what could be improved.

FP: Which project was it that brought you into closer contact?

KG: The Muji/Thonet project was probably the one on which we worked most closely. Muji wanted to reinterpret Thonet's two most iconic products: the famous Chair No. 14 in bentwood and Marcel Breuer's tubular steel furniture. At the time, James was working as art director for Thonet. He not only established the connection between Muji and Thonet, he also handled most of the communication between the two companies and followed the technical development process of our projects. It was not an easy task and without James the project would never have worked. He was someone who had this extraordinary capacity to connect with people and to win over their heart for a cause. That was his role in the Muji/Thonet project for sure. On many other occasions I noticed this side of him: James could have a relationship with all sorts of people and all sorts of situations. He could bring something magic out of people.

FP: How did you tackle this project when it involves such icons of design?

KG: As designers, how could we deal with Thonet's heritage? We talked a lot about how to approach the project in the right way, and to find the proper balance between changing things and leaving them the way they were: treating them with due respect,

Irvine with the Thonet family at the Milan Furniture Fair stand he designed in 2005

At the presentation of prototypes for Grcic's Muji-Thonet Pipe Desk, taken by Irvine, 2009 (L-R: Naoto Fukasawa, Konstantin Grcic and Masaaki Kanai, president of Muji)

but also with the confidence to say 'today we do things differently'. On this project James and I were totally thinking along the same lines. It was a very strong experience, and eventually very rewarding. It was definitively down to James that the whole project worked.

I learned so much from James just by listening to him. Having a conversation with him always had great value, because he was so open and generous – he would share what he knew and offer advice. I'm normally shy when asking for advice, but James opened that door to me and I knew I could ask his advice about anything: money, contacts, companies – anything. Anyway, James was a great storyteller. And his famous jokes! He always had a joke to tell. Whether they were funny or not – most of them were – I would bend over laughing just by the way he told it. I'm sure many other people would say the same thing about their friendship with James. It's what made him so special to so many people. He was able to have very personal relationships with a lot of very different people. He made everyone feel very easy and close.

FP: Looking back through James's sketches, we find many references to human features – the object being represented as a person. That 'animistic' element is very clear in his studies for furniture feet, to which he always paid great attention, as in the design of the Piceno chair. In the sketches for the desk fan for Muji, he incorporated a smile motif into the design of the knob. Do you think all that can be connected

with a shift from the idea of function towards a more personal relationship with objects, from a post-modern viewpoint?

KG: When you mention the smile in the design of the knob, I believe that is still a function. I mean that James and his generation became very aware of the emotional value of objects – that an object is not just a practical thing, it is something you build a relationship with. This idea definitely comes from the post-modern movement, and I think it expanded our understanding of what a function is. I think we are all functionalists, but in a broader sense.

FP: Do you think that this kind of emotional value that James attributed to objects is something that could also be described by his passion for collecting things?

KG: James liked to collect things but in a funny way. He was in love with all sorts of crazy little toys and manga comics – and of course he was mad about cars and motorbikes. James totally had his own way of – what today we might call – 'curating' objects, if that doesn't sound too pretentious. He had a real kind of affection for things.

FP: Do you also share this collecting habit with him?

KG: I end up surrounding myself with things I like, but I'm not a collector. Of course I have a passion for things, but I am never obsessive about it. Even James was not obsessed with objects. He was playful with his collections – he enjoyed them. He needed the stimulus of these new things: finding them, keeping them and taking comfort from them.

James always kept a boyish side in him, staying a kid – and I mean that in a nice way. Not like an adult who doesn't want to grow up, but in the way he looked at the world, his curiosity, playfulness and humour. James was a positive person – he believed in a good world, even though he became very critical about the disasters of modern society and the political climate (especially in the Italy of the Berlusconi era). It was in his character to enjoy things, and to be positive. I think this is obvious in his designs: they are optimistic, and add something beautiful to people's lives, something they can enjoy.

FP: This reminds me of something Dostoevsky wrote about beauty and the fact that it 'will save the world'.

Worker at the marble quarry used for Marsotto's projects, 2012

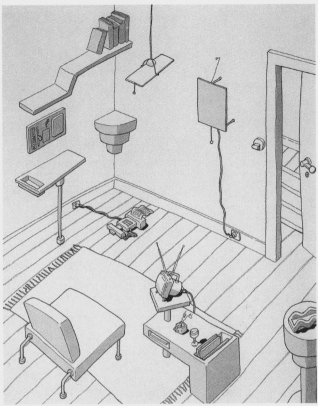

Drawing for Japanese project, 1989

I would like to conclude by talking about the project for Marsotto. To what extent do you think that a project like this, that James wanted to share with all of you, could be considered in its own way visionary?

KG: What mattered to us about working with this company was that our heart was fully in it. It is a joy to work with that kind of industry and with people like Costanza Olfi and Mario Marsotto. Maybe it's a dream, a romantic idea, but it matters and that makes it worth it. Of course it would be great to earn money with all these beautiful works, but you can't exchange this for anything. The product would not be the same for a gallery. It's the whole story – that's what it's about.

The story of a company like Marsotto, what they do, the craftsmanship, the idea of a typical Italian family business, the business itself, which acts like an editor, designing a product and not an art piece – I believe that was James's real motivation, in re-visiting the old model. And in the end I don't think it is out-dated, because it represents a situation of today's market. I think we experienced globalization and realized that doing projects for companies on the other side of the world can be quite frustrating.

FP: Really? Why?

KG: Because everything that's important about designing, about working on a project, it all gets lost: the proximity, the discourse, the passion. It's not the same, communicating through Skype.

FP: But doesn't the world that you're talking about seem doomed to disappear within a few years?

KG: That's why it matters even more to save it, to keep it alive. I think James thought that way, and I think we are all putting our time and effort into projects like Marsotto because we believe that there is something precious about it that has to be preserved.

FP: It's kind of a romantic approach isn't it?

KG: Totally. But being the designers we are is romantic. Designing products is romantic. The collective spirit generated by projects like the one James created for Marsotto is romantic. Why not. Isn't that a beautiful thing?

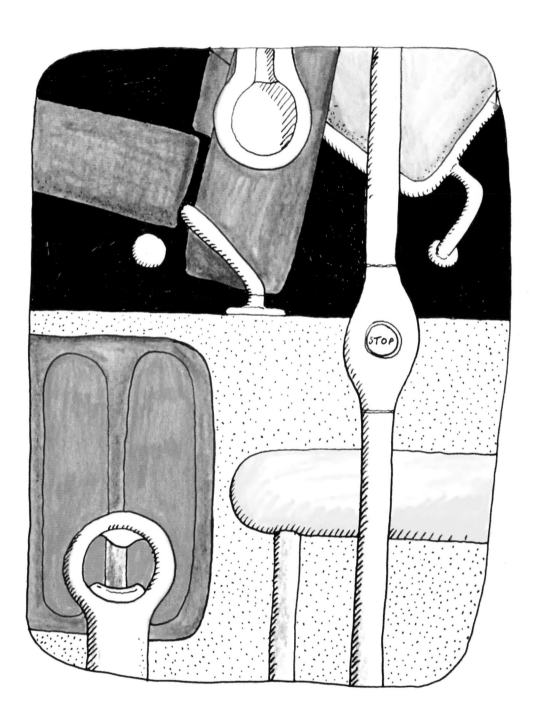

PRACTICAL PEOPLE WHO LIKE TO SOLVE PROBLEMS

TO MR. MARC NEWSON.

HEY MARC.
HAVE A
GREAT NIGHT.
VROOM VROOM

Fax sent by Irvine to Marc Newson, 1996

FRANCESCA PICCHI: Can you help us trace the story of your relationship with James, along with the projects and experiences that you shared together?

MARC NEWSON: I first met James in the early 1990s, along with Jasper Morrison. We had all started working with a variety of Italian furniture companies, specifically the likes of Cappellini, with whom we all worked a lot in the early days. We became friends immediately and James became a kind of focus in Milan, where he already lived back then. Our interactions were in fact mostly personal and not professional, although we clearly had a lot in common work-wise.

Other close friends we shared were the Swedish architects Peter Hallen and Thomas Sandell and designers Stefano Giovannoni and Fabrice Domercq (who now makes wine with Jasper). James, Fabrice and I actually shared a fantastic villa right on the shores of Lake Como in the small town of Torno, and I have very fond memories of weekends spent there. There was certainly a lot of food and drink, and the occasional waterskiing session in front of the Villa

Silva – James on water skis is an image that will forever stick in my mind!

FP: It seems that you not only shared a common vision of design but also your everyday social lives. Obviously you spent much of your free time together at the villa, not to mention Bar Basso… I don't know if you could be classified a design movement, but certainly you can be identified as group of friends who have a lot in common. How much of your design was collaborative? Do you remember any discussion or topic in particular that you debated together?

MN: The wonderful thing is that I can't ever remember discussing design once! Our shared villa represented an opportunity to meet and have fun together but its particular geographical location was somewhat incidental, despite being extraordinarily beautiful. In some ways I recall we almost actively avoided talking about design, except when experiencing moments of hardship, which was certainly very often in those days!

FP: In the early 1990s, James and Jasper involved you in the Progetto Oggetto project for Cappellini, marking the start of a new generation of designers. Can you help to define the common spirit that linked the design approach of all these different designers?

MN: To be honest, when you're in the midst of such a 'moment', one doesn't think about the greater implications of what is being created in terms of a movement. It was a case of attracting like-minded people, who could collaborate easily together without the risk of egos becoming dominant. In short, it was more about creating an excuse to have some fun and potentially create a body of work that was greater than the sum of all its pieces. Giulio (Cappellini) was of course also instrumental in facilitating the project – the idea of which was inevitably more ambitious than its reality. But we were all relatively young back then, had lots of energy and certainly more time…

FP: Of this group of iconic designers, you are arguably the one who has explored the relationship between art and design, between edition and production and between the art market and the mass market, in the most striking and extreme way. Your pieces in marble for Gagosian or the Lockheed Lounge completely changed the perception of design and its potential in the market. On the other hand,

PRACTICAL PEOPLE WHO LIKE TO SOLVE PROBLEMS

126

At the villa on Lake Como, early 1990s

James's marble pieces for Marsotto endured the almost romantic idea of working with small industrial companies. Did you ever talk with James about this change in the perception of the industrial object in a society that is now post-industrial?

MN: No, I never really spoke directly to James about this, but there was always an unspoken, implicit acknowledgment and respect for the differing ways with which we had had attempted to solve similar problems, or at least address our mutual desires; which was ultimately to try and produce beautiful pieces. More importantly, in the specific case of marble, I think we both loved the idea of working with a somewhat anachronistic material and the potential to reintroduce it to an unexpecting audience. Of course now that may seem presumptuous, but in 2005 when I first started producing these pieces in marble, it was seen as strange to say the least.

FP: Your generation, which emerged in the 1990s, shared a common belief about working with industry and mass-market products. Your perception of industry must have changed, in the same way that today's industrial landscape itself has deeply changed. What do you think is different now about your position as a designer?

MN: I think that fundamentally my position as a designer has not changed (and I'm sure it was the same for James). Perhaps at certain moments the perception has been that of change, but I remain confident that my ability to move swiftly through different mediums and expressions illustrates a certain versatility. I perceive this as a positive and valuable

attribute for a designer, as we must constantly embrace change.

FP: Your decision to join a great company like Apple could be seen as part of today's different approach to industry. All the designers of your generation (just like the old maestros of the post-War era) founded their own personal studios, which independently collaborated with different industries and companies. Do you think that this kind of model no longer works, due to the growing complexity of industrial products? Did you ever talk about it with James?

MN: No, I never talked about this with James, but he was always a huge fan of Apple! To be clear, I am now working with Apple but I also retain my own studio and preserve my own clients. It's an extremely unusual situation, but again I don't perceive boundaries in terms of understanding new ways of working. At the end of the day, we want to create great products or objects, and the method by which we do this should be a means to an end. For me, convention does not dictate a particular way that I should or shouldn't work; all possibilities remain open.

FP: You and James shared an early experience in Japan during the 1980s. How do you think you both were influenced by Japan?

MN: James and I were indeed both incredibly influenced by Japan. We both lived there for short periods but travelled, over the years extensively back to Japan. As a source of inspiration (and amusement, because we constantly tried to out-do each other with our faux Japanese accents!), Japan was quite simply second to none; it somehow figured in every conversation we had.

Perhaps the single greatest pleasure in Tokyo for both of us remained the ritualistic visit to Tokyu Hands, the best department store in the world. Of course it has now achieved a kind of cult status, but in the mid-late 1980s it was an obscure reference that acted as a bond between people. If James could be awarded a posthumous honour from them, it would surely have been one of his significant achievements!

FP: James went to Milan to work as a product designer for Olivetti – which at that time was a very advanced company. When he was in Japan working for Toshiba, he conceived very advanced experimental

Motorbike sketch, early 1990s

projects, for example he designed a concept for a computer that looks like an iPad long before it was invented. Did he ever talk with you about his experience at Olivetti or Toshiba?

MN: Yes, we discussed his experiences in Japan many times, not least because James and I lived both lived there a long time ago and the place remained a huge source of inspiration to both of us. James had a very rare type of personality that enabled him to blend in with completely foreign cultures. Like me, I felt that he never had any issue working with large technological companies, like Olivetti or Toshiba. He was also aware of the fact that Olivetti had produced truly iconic products, and that they championed the importance of design, much like Apple does today.

FP: In the early 1990s, Cappellini produced one of your first works — the Orgone chaise longue. The very name of this chair is a reference to a energetic vision of life — the word 'orgone' was in fact, coined by a peculiar figure, Wilhelm Reich, an Austrian psychoanalyst disciple of Sigmund Frued, whose bio-energetic theory influenced generations of intellectuals and also the hippy culture during the 1960s. Through his research, the Orgone Energy Devices were developed — supposedly able to catch any negative energy that surrounds a person and transform it into a happier and more positive mood. I think this idea of the presence of energy within objects, influencing our relationship with them is something that I can detect, in different measures, hidden in the background of all your works.

        Some years ago, Jasper made a reference to the psychoanalysis of an object, thinking about objects as presences with a personality. James himself used to sketch his objects with human characters — almost like a kind of animistic presence hidden within them. Do you think that this idea of an object containing a kind of energy with the power to positively influence people, could be seen as a different approach to

designing beyond the idea of function? But first of all, where did this 'orgone' reference come from?

MN: The 'orgone' reference did indeed come from an obsession with Wilhelm Reich that I developed during my time at art school. Personalities like his were seen as topical and it was definitely one of the nice things about going to art school, as opposed to design school, which didn't seem to be as concerned with esoteric issues. However, my interest in Reich was not necessarily concerned with particular devices like the Orgone box, but more with the fact that he was a visionary who worked on a vast number of differing projects, from cloud busters to psychotherapy. I loved the idea of this maverick attempting to do such a mad variety of controversial things, which he was inevitably persecuted for.

        Subconsciously, there was very definitely an element of imbuing my pieces with a kind of personality. I remember creating my first Lockheed Lounge and having a strange out-of-body experience at the moment it was born, like a transfer of energy (or life force!) that brought it into reality, a bit like Frankenstein's monster... It happened on several occasions, and to a lesser degree it still happens with a lot of what I do.

FP: You are considered to have a strong organic approach to form and design — as was James. There was a period that James used to refer to as his 'sausage' period, when his visual vocabulary was based on this rounded 'sausage-like' form. At the same time your vocabulary revolved around the idea of the pod: how would you describe your common — or different — approaches to these organic forms?

MN: I've never been that comfortable with the 'organic' label, however in the absence of a better description I have accepted to live with it. The problem for me with organic is that it implies a sense of randomness that is absolutely never present in my work. I believe, as I'm certain James did, that parameters like symmetry, balance and harmony were far more important in determining the underlying character of a piece. Sausages and pods could certainly be classed as organic but they are also generally well organised!

FP: Transport and travelling have been a constant theme in your work. You and James shared a strong passion for cars, motorbikes, (he designed a bus and you aeroplane interiors) and all that is connected to this mechanical world. Can you tell us a little more about this common passion and the way it influenced your design?

MN: Perhaps this mutual obsession has to do with a couple of distinct things. Firstly, I think it was a constant reminder to one's own childhood and preserving the importance of reference in our daily lives. I think its true to say that both James and I shared the philosophy that 'we worked to live' and not the inverse, however if the opportunity existed to combine both (cars and bikes for example), then all the better.

The other important concern is that our understanding of the mechanical world is driven and inspired by complex, beautiful engineering. James shared a wonderful, enormous and clean garage space with our great mutual friend Joel Berg in Milan. This place was a haven, perhaps even sacred. It's what he dreamt of having and the one thing I have lusted for all of my life!

FP: What do you think you shared the most with James from the point of view of your design approach?

MN: It's very hard to say, but it would be something very simple, and perhaps something that didn't obviously have anything to do with design approach. Like I alluded to before, I feel both James and I are enormously practical people who just like to solve problems, and I think this remains clear.

Stand-by modular seating system for Mabeg, 2001

Atom carpet design for Nodus, 2009

MARC NEWSON

I remember well the moment that James
called me up to help him out on the
Hanover bus project for üstra, the city's
public transport operator. James was
extremely busy with his work as design
director at Sottsass Associati, and
was pursuing a large number of projects
with his own studio. He travelled
endlessly, but had the stamina of
a team of English footballers.

Despite our hectic schedules, we would
meet first thing in the morning, James
would make some sketches, and then head
off to Ettore's. He would rush back at
lunch, make a few comments, feverishly
sketch (always with his characteristic
'grin and glint') and then off he went
again. Running out the door, he would
say things like, 'Remember, make the
door bigger, in case couples need to get
on and off, hand in hand!' At aperitivo
time, James would be back in the office,
drink in hand, to review the day's work.

That was a typical day, usually ending
with a dinner with friends and then
sketching late into the evening. James
had this ability to be everywhere at
the same time. In fact, he was the
epicentre of many crossing paths. He
brought opposing approaches, continents,
friends, clients and designers together
seamlessly. - Tim Power

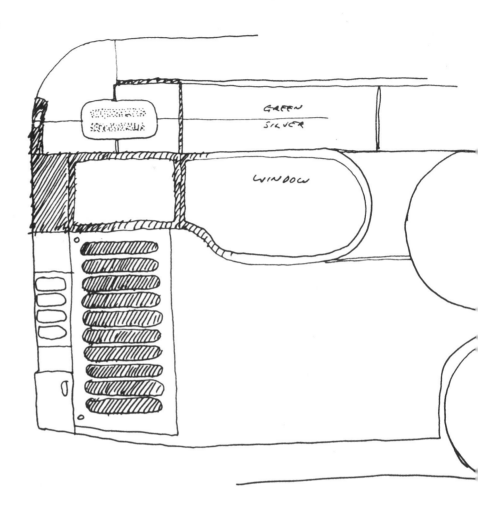

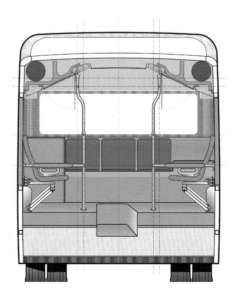

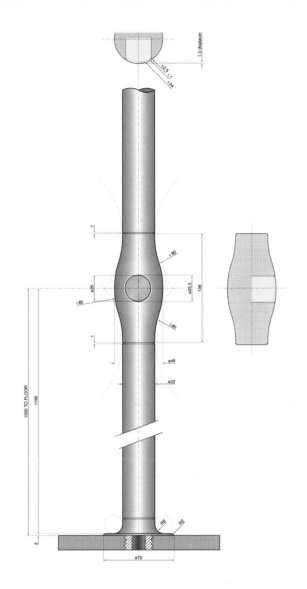

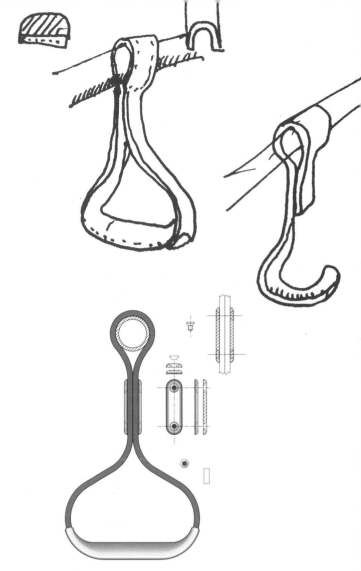

In 2000, Canon asked me to design a fax machine
for home use. Since they wanted to concentrate
on the European market, they thought they would
involve a number of European designers. Two other
proposals, by their in-house designers, were drawn
up alongside mine. The proposals were shown to
members of the public in London, Paris and Milan,
who were asked to choose their favourite: my
designs scored 90% of the votes in London, 87%
in Paris and 88% in Milan.

They couldn't believe it, but the result was
clear. The idea of suggesting a silver finish -
which at the time was only used for hi-fi products
- was seen by the European market as adding
value. It was an enjoyable experience, but with
the rise of e-mail, fax slowly became obsolete.
Nevertheless, the model remained in production
from 2000 to 2004. - James Irvine

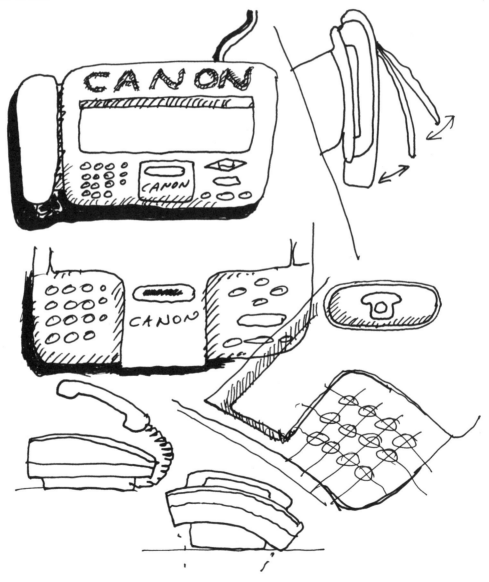

Microwaves have been designed as a box for many years, for good
reason. Boxes, however, can be designed in hundreds of ways,
so I didn't feel that the box was a limitation but rather
something to be respected. One of the great characteristics
of the microwave is that it is a self-contained product
and therefore can be installed anywhere. You just plug it in.
But who might plug it in and where?

Toshiki and Keiko have a very small kitchen in their apartment
in Roppongi, Tokyo. Toshiki nearly always works late. Keiko leaves
him a little bowl of soup, which he heats up when he gets home
and drinks while listening to the midnight news.

Cindy is a shy girl. In fact, she likes to stay in her room and
read romantic novels. She asked her parents to buy her a microwave
for Christmas so that she doesn't have to go up and down stairs
all the time.

Colette and Jules have a small restaurant, which unfortunately
does not have a star in the Michelin guide. They discovered that
a microwave is very handy for defrosting the escargot.

Pete, Clive and Sam are students and they share a small flat in
Earls Court, London. The kitchen is always filthy. They never cook,
but sometimes they need to re-heat some left over Indian take away.
- James Irvine

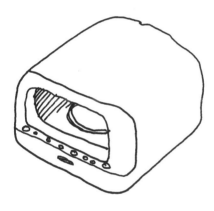

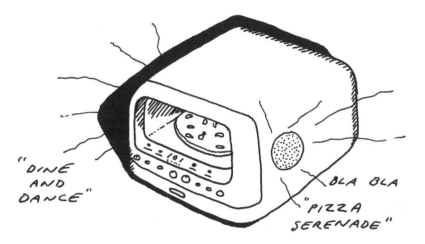

1. FLOAT

The idea behind the design of Float was to make the object invisible and the light visible. Ernesto Gismondi (the founder of Artemide) came to see the paperboard model we had made in the studio. He liked it a lot and immediately decided to put it into production: a good example of the clear thinking of Italian industrialists! - James Irvine

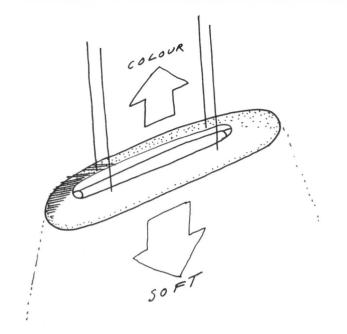

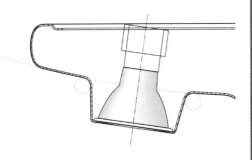

2. ONE TWO

A multipurpose lamp that transforms
indirect light, which illuminates
the whole space, into direct light,
that can be pointed in different
directions simply by turning the
'stem', to create light that is
precise and sharply focused.

The circular aluminium diffusor can
be adjusted on its vertical axis;
a small movement of the hand on
the notch underneath controls the
intensity of light falling directly
on the work-surface. - James Irvine

1. SONIA

Sonia is one of those chairs that
I have always dreamt of designing:
a wooden chair that stacks. The idea
of Sonia is that visually it looks
like a single sheet. Just like the
paper models you make at design
school. - James Irvine

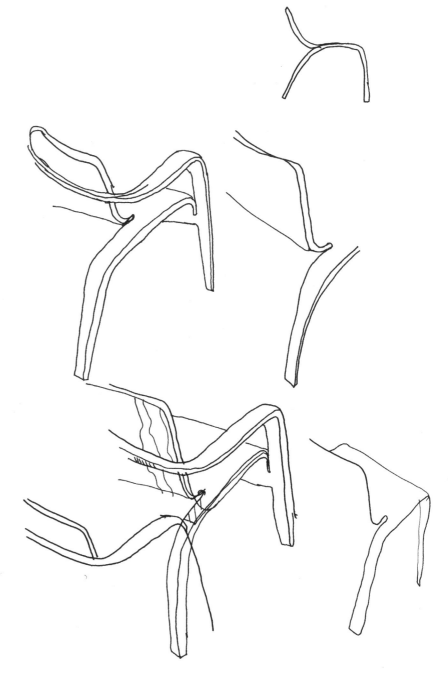

2. X3 TABLE

Flat-pack tray table, which can
be easily assembled and stored

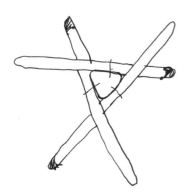

Like any typical industrial designer, I wanted
to control the glass and design precise forms with
precise shapes. But glass doesn't work like that,
so the surprise of the randomness of each form
is in fact a pleasure for me. Every single one
is slightly different. - James Irvine

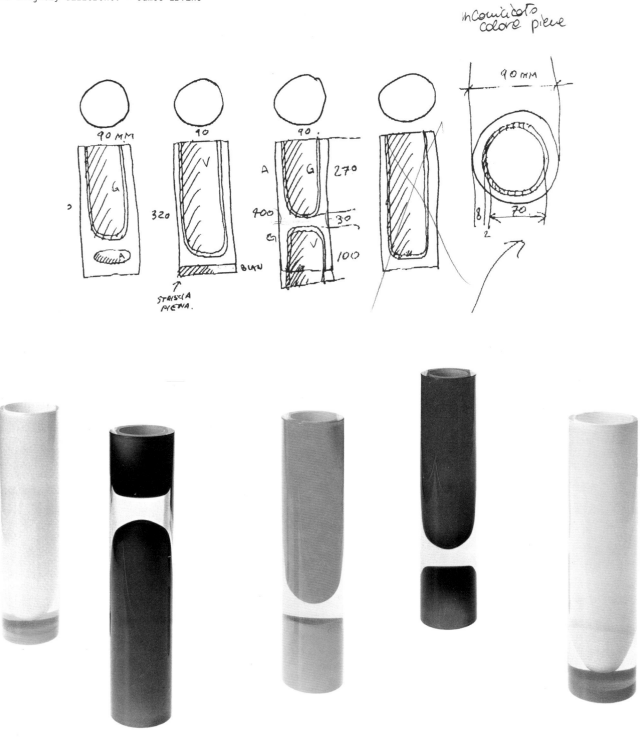

Pots, plates and containers for growing herbs
and vegetables that you can then serve directly
on your table. It is a pleasure to see seeds
sprout and shoots grow. Not to mention you
know exactly what your own produce contains.
- James Irvine

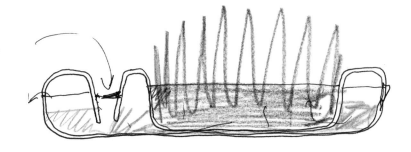

1. ARCHIVIO VIVO (2001)

When I decided to relaunch the Danese
brand in order to revive a tradition that
originated in the work of Bruno Munari and
Enzo Mari, I immediately thought of James,
whose work I admired so much and of which
I am a devoted collector. One of his
first pieces for the new collection was a
shelving system in extruded aluminium,
thought of as a flexible means of displaying
important things and keeping them within
sight. - Carlotta de Bevilacqua

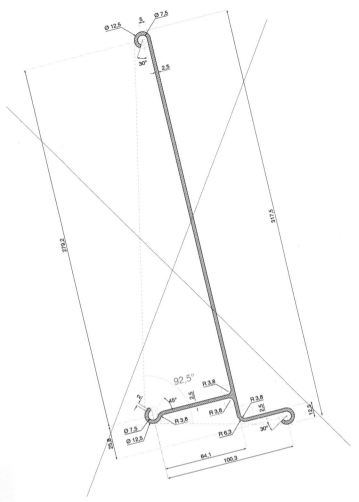

2. BIG SUPERHOOK / BIG FIVE (2001)

James also produced a collection of small,
brightly coloured objects, including
a series of clothes hooks, using a new type
of adhesive developed by 3M that avoided
drilling holes in the wall. I believe
James wrote a new chapter in the history
of industrial design and I consider it
a privilege to have worked with him.
- Carlotta de Bevilacqua

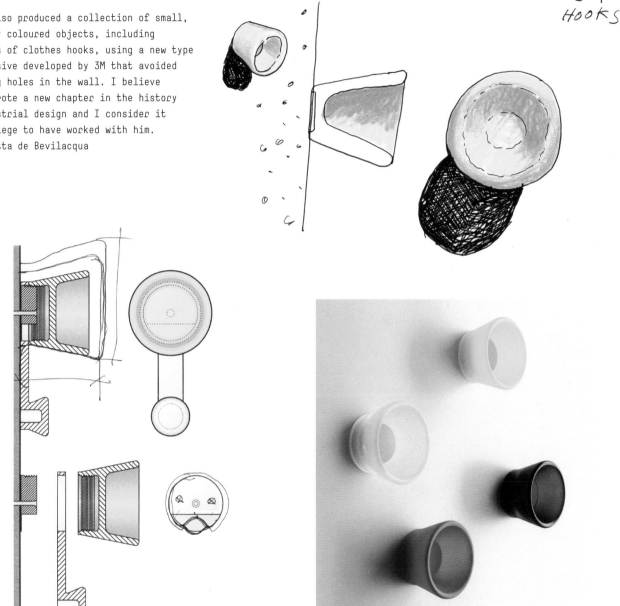

3M
HOOKS

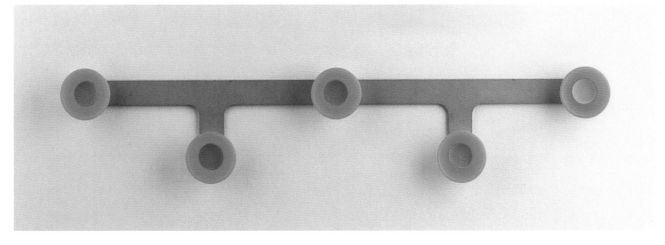

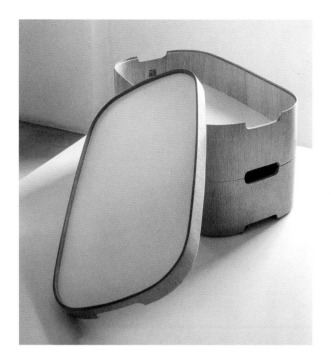

3. HOLD IT (2002)

I have always been fanatical about having a place to store things. All those things that must be put somewhere, but you never quite know where. I love drawers, but then drawers are fairly static - unless they are on wheels. But even then, it is rare to be able to pull out a drawer and use it as a portable box. The purpose of Hold It depends on the imagination of the user. As a tower of boxes, it becomes a kind of archive.

Each box could be for specific things or just a complete mess. Then the final lid becomes a tray so as to offer people the treasures the box may hold. So, who could use Hold It? My mother might use it for her knitting wool; my younger brother would perhaps use it for his tool kit; my father might use it for his socks and underpants and I am absolutely sure that my nephew would use Hold It for his Lego bricks. I think I might use Hold It for all my maps from my journeys around the world. What would you use it for? - James Irvine

4. MAKE UP (2007)

The name of this product reflects just one of its many functions - for use when applying make up. The mirror has a recessed shelf where you can keep your lipstick, mascara, tweezers etc. You can hang it near the entrance for that last-minute touch-up before leaving. A bit of lipstick, a touch of mascara, a brush-stroke of blusher and so on.

If the shelf is not crowded with make-up paraphernalia, you can also use it to store your mail, keys, mobile phone and other unisex objects. In fact this mirror is not just for women, since men often love to have a quick look at themselves too... - James Irvine

5. BELVEDERE (2006)

If you flick through an atlas - one of those that uses pastel colours - you immediately see the shape of each country: some are beautiful, some are ugly. Some are interesting, others are boring. Italy has the fortune of being a 'beautiful country'. It is not really fair to call it 'the boot'. For me it seems more like a leg. A leg which is rather beautiful.

Where could you hang this mirror? In a pizzeria, in a travel agency or in the foyer of an important Italian company where it might be useful for a beautiful girl to put on her lipstick.
- James Irvine

IN-CUBO

James Irvine

www.in-cubo.com

6. DAISY (2004)

There are many coat stands in the world.
Most of them work very well. Most, will
accept six coats, just like Daisy.
However, coat stands - like most objects
- are sometimes empty, with no coats.
Then they become objects which are not
just purely functional, you have to look
at them, they hang around waiting. Daisy
is waiting. - James Irvine

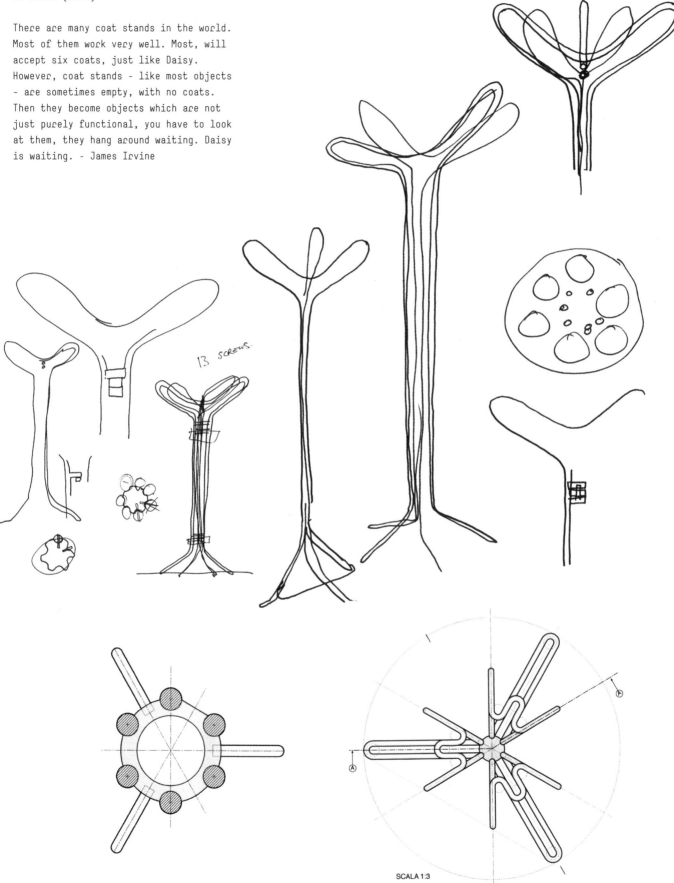

13 screws.

SCALA 1:3

DANESE / Daisy

... Geflügelscheere, Käsemühle, Kräutermühle, Knoblauchpresse, Flaschenöffner, Aschenbecher, Weinkühler, Butterdose, Fleischklopfer, Eierbecher, Folienschneider, Korkenzieher, Salatschüssel, Eiskübel... the lists of objects to design for WMF went on, and on and on.

James loved designing for WMF. This was real industrial design - mass production - and you'll find these objects in every household in Germany (as he liked to explain). He also loved the material - stainless steel - cool and timeless. However, unlike his predecessors who underlined the 'sheet' with their designs, James didn't always follow the laws of economic material usage and processes. He preferred to create objects with complete volumes - pleasant to look at and pleasant to touch. In some cases this was achieved purely through visual effects (no sheet edges are visible) but often two halves had to be welded together, or very thick sheet material had to be used - sometimes it was even cast. Think about all the polishing! And yes, James was right - years after these objects were designed it is wonderful to re-discover them in friends' drawers, as good as new, and to remember the time of their development. - Dunja Weber

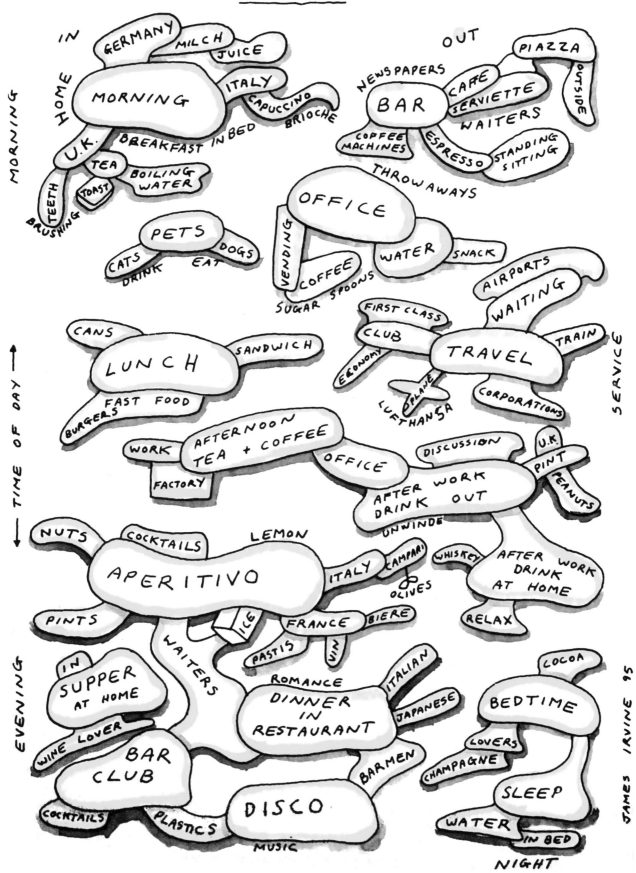

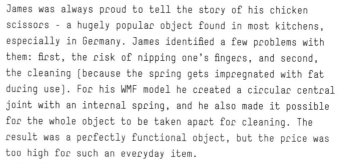
WMF.
"CHICKEN SCISSORS"
TORNO 13.08.96.

James was always proud to tell the story of his chicken scissors - a hugely popular object found in most kitchens, especially in Germany. James identified a few problems with them: first, the risk of nipping one's fingers, and second, the cleaning (because the spring gets impregnated with fat during use). For his WMF model he created a circular central joint with an internal spring, and he also made it possible for the whole object to be taken apart for cleaning. The result was a perfectly functional object, but the price was too high for such an everyday item.
- Marialaura Rossiello Irvine

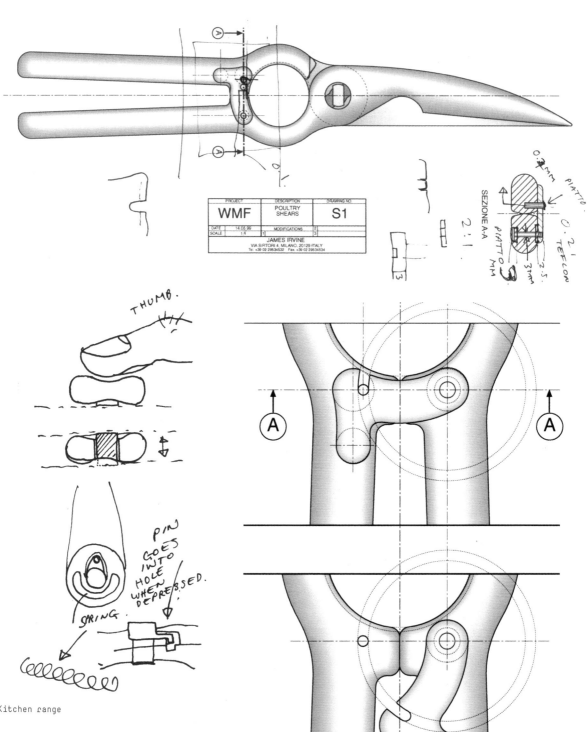

PROJECT	DESCRIPTION	DRAWING NO.
WMF	POULTRY SHEARS	S1

| DATE | 14.08.99 | MODIFICATIONS | 2 |
| SCALE | 1:1 | | 3 |

JAMES IRVINE
VIA SIRTORI 4, MILANO, 20129 ITALY
Tel. +39 02 29534532   Fax +39 02 29534534

SEZIONE A-A   2:1.

THUMB.

PIN GOES INTO HOLE WHEN DEPRESSED.

SPRING.

When Massimiliano Yien asked me to design a pen
for A.G. Spalding & Bros., I thought: what a
wonderful project, but what can I do? Surely it has
all been done before. So I designed the most simple
'disappearing' pen possible, but when it came to
the clip, I needed a special idea. I realized that
to make the pen even simpler, I wanted the clip
to disappear too. We developed a clip on a spring
mechanism. In this way it stays flush with the
body of the pen so that the form is clean in one's
hand. There is a button to push out the clip on
the back of the pen.

The other advantage of the clip is that by pushing
the button, you can free it totally from the fabric
of the pocket in a simple, one-handed movement.
It may not seem like much, but how many of us have
ripped pockets in our jackets from nasty clips on
pens? I certainly have, have you? - James Irvine.

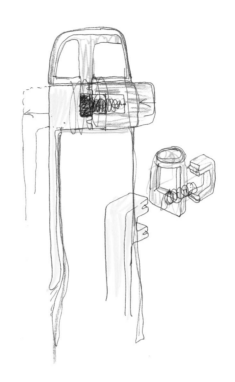

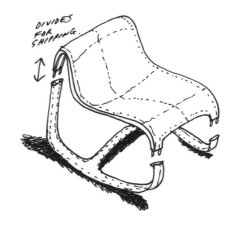

At a conference on Scandinavian design organized by
the Swedish Embassy, which James attended in New
York, one of the main topics of discussion was the
environment. Since James was rather critical of Ikea's
'fast consumption' policy, his arguments attracted
the attention of Ikea's design director, Lars Engman.
After the conference, Engman introduced himself,
and to James's great surprise, invited him to design
specifically for Ikea. Thus began a collaboration to
design a chair made in China using rattan, a natural
material with low environmental impact, woven by hand
around a steel frame. - Sabrina Sciama

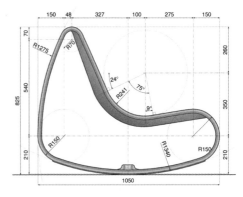

VITAMIN BAR, DU PONT CORIAN • 2003

One thing characteristic of trade fairs is the constant battle to get a drink. Interminable queues for a glass of cheap prosecco. Is all this healthy? Not really. Would you prefer something that gives you stamina, strength or vitality? I am not sure about that either, but if it is better than cheap prosecco, then why not?

So in this I found my own brief. The project needed to be big, sociable, healthy, illuminated and give the opportunity for a moment of relaxation. How big? As big as possible. How many people? Sixteen is a nice number. What kind of light? Mysterious, with changing colours. What should we serve our tired friends to drink? A strange coloured liquid which is good for you. What is in the liquid? Now that's a secret.

The other day I was watching TV and suddenly realized that the 'Vitamin Bar' looks rather similar to the giant meeting table at the United Nations. What a lucky coincidence for me... - James Irvine

4 ZETA
+
TAVOLO CON
PIATTI E VINO.

CORTILE
AL APERTO
CON SOLE
E PIANTE
TIPO RINGHIERA.
"LA VECCHIA MILANO".

CANNA DEL'ACQUA
MAGARI ARANCIA
O GIALLA.
ANCHE UNA SCOPA
O UNA PERSONA.
CHE CAVA.

This outdoor collection consists of
a zeta ('zed') shaped stacking chair
and a flat-pack table in both a square
and round version

FRANKFURT BOOK FAIR STAND, PHAIDON PRESS • 2003

We commissioned James to design a new stand that would
represent the Phaidon brand and what it stands for, at
the most important book fair in the world. After having
looked at what publishers were doing, he started asking
us some basic questions: why, when we wanted to showcase
and celebrate our books, did we close them within walls?
Why did we use dark wood for the shelves, when it meant
that the books didn't stand out? Why did we rely on the
limited lighting system of the fair?

And then he came up with some brilliant solutions: the
stand would be completely open, so that people would feel
invited, and welcome to look at the books. The space
would be defined simply by a white, slightly raised floor
- white would be the main colour against which the books
stand out in all their beauty, with some hints of colour
provided by the orange for the electric system running
through the floor, and the grey and orange curtains that
define the meeting rooms. And finally, the books would be
the heroes of the stand - displayed face out, both on
shelves and tables, cleverly lit by a hidden lighting
system. - Emilia Terragni

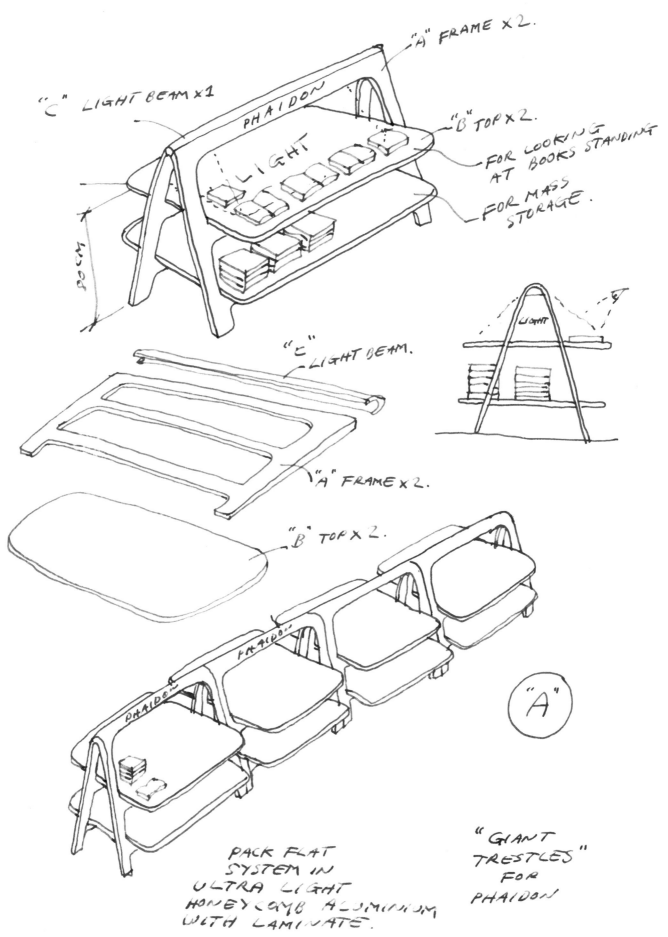

"A" FRAME x2.

"C" LIGHT BEAM x1

PHAIDON

LIGHT

"B" TOP x2.

FOR LOOKING AT BOOKS STANDING

FOR MASS STORAGE.

90CM

"C" LIGHT BEAM.

LIGHT

"A" FRAME x2.

"B" TOP x2.

PHAIDON

PHAIDON

PHAIDON

"A"

PACK FLAT SYSTEM IN ULTRA LIGHT HONEYCOMB ALUMINIUM WITH LAMINATE.

"GIANT TRESTLES" FOR PHAIDON

When Antonio Olivari first contacted me, I recall feeling
intimidated. Olivari, the world-famous makers of handles
and door-knobs, who had worked with so many big names! How
does one design a handle for such a prestigious company?
I started making sketches, keeping them to myself. To begin
with, they were weird ideas, and when I looked at them,
I wondered if I really wanted a handle like that. To tell the
truth, I didn't. Perhaps the handle didn't always have to
be the star of the show. Perhaps it could be quite simple.
The kind of thing you sketch when you have to draw a
pictogram of a handle: a handle, not a flower, a spaceship
or part of an engine. The more simply I drew it, the more
I liked it. Then I had the idea of filling it out a little,
so that it looked even more cartoonish. When Antonio asked
me, 'What shall we call it?' I said it reminded me of the
Olivari logo, and Antonio replied, 'Then Logo it shall be!'
- James Irvine

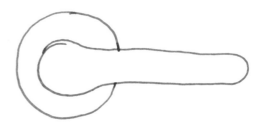

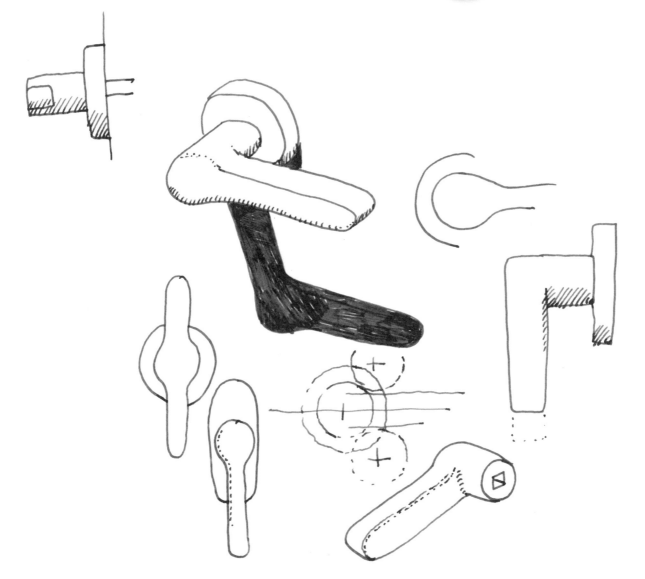

The great thing about working with Kreo, is that you can really experiment. By this I mean create objects or pieces of furniture that would never be made by normal industry. Out of the normal logic. This does not mean that what one creates is not useful. On the contrary, the object can be 'extra' useful because one can design out of the system and usually systems mean things have to be standardized. Thus, the distance between shelves on a bookcase tends to be a nice, logical distance and more or less always the same.

CASINO FOR KREO

But our lives are full of many different objects with many different forms. Tall, wide, short and fat. *Casino* means 'mess' in Italian. So for our messy lives with messy things we need an object that itself is rather disordered. Disorder for disorder to create order. *Un bel Casino.* - James Irvine

1. LOOP CHAIR (2004)

In 2004, Philipp Thonet - one of three brothers in the fifth generation of the German family - came to my studio in Milan. I couldn't believe that I was meeting a genuine Thonet! A 'living treasure', as the Japanese would call him. We became friends, and the Thonet brand is now part of who I am. Back then, on that first occasion, when he asked me to design a bentwood chair, I replied, 'impossible!'

But a year later, in a bar in Cologne, the concept of the Loop chair came to me: a single line joining the back and the seat, like a large bent tennis racket. The design combines the traditional warmth of wood with the lightness and comfort of modern materials, but the chair's real innovation is in the curvature of the wood. When you look at it, you immediately see how simple it is.
- James Irvine

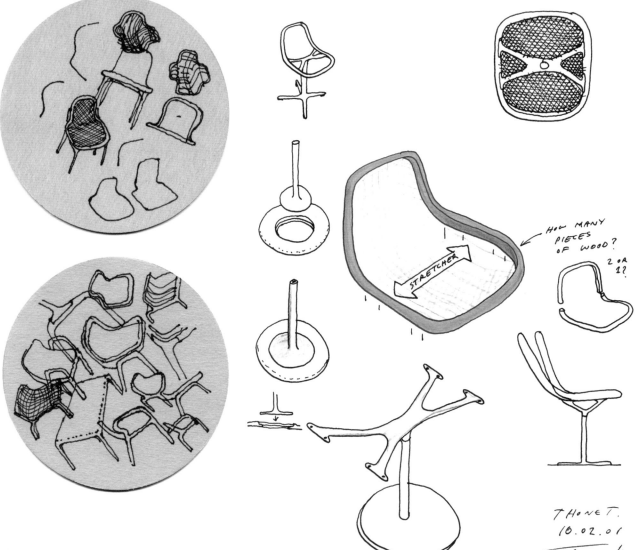

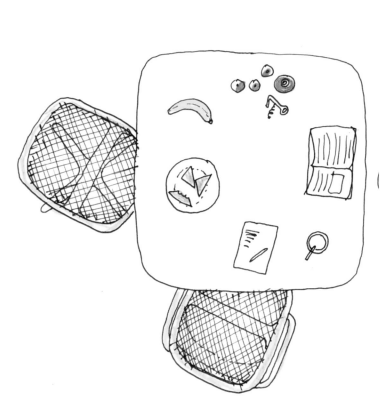

THONET / Loop chair

2. S5000 SOFA (2006)

The S5000 is a new interpretation
of a sofa that appeared in the Thonet
catalogue back in the 1930s - the
archetype of the minimalist sofa,
with a steel tube base. The Thonet
tradition provides the designer
with a language and an approach to
construction that are timeless. After
working with Thonet for years, I now
understand that it is possible to re-
invent products that are perhaps even
better suited to our times.
- James Irvine

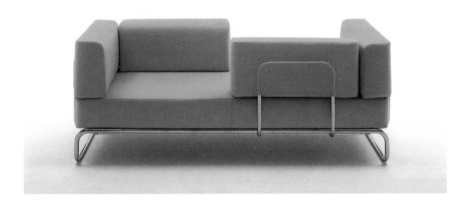

In this metal coat stand reminiscent of a cactus, the twelve hooks protrude as if the whole piece has been folded out of cardboard. - Francesca Picchi

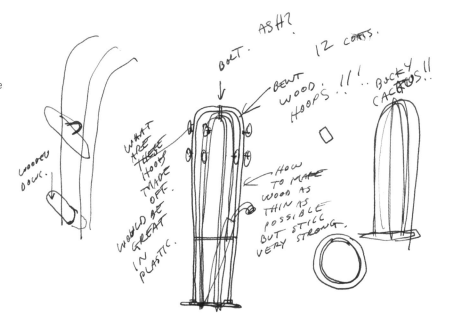

When Olivetti decided to develop a printer, they entered a very difficult market - competing with brands that were unbeatable in terms of price and distribution. I discussed the project with Alberto, and we decided to go for something different, thinking about how we could create something that was currently missing from that market. Printers are basically boxes that dispense rectangular sheets of paper, which end up on tables cluttered with other things that are often also rectangular. It's not clear why they should have these excessively bulky, graphic, obtrusive and ultimately meaningless shapes. They're all the same and it hardly matters what's inside. To break into this market, we chose a 'purist' strategy - to put across a message of diversity.

The market forces you to copy what sells, with minor changes dictated by marketing, and not by the real possibility of developing the product further. Hardly anyone says, 'let's start from scratch'. With the Olivetti printers we tried, I wouldn't say we started from scratch, but instead posed the question of what might be placed next to the machine: it could be anything, even my grandmother's coloured glass vase. In the end, there are objects made to be seen - 'centre-stage' objects - and others made to do things. We also have to learn to appreciate design that doesn't take centre-stage. - James Irvine

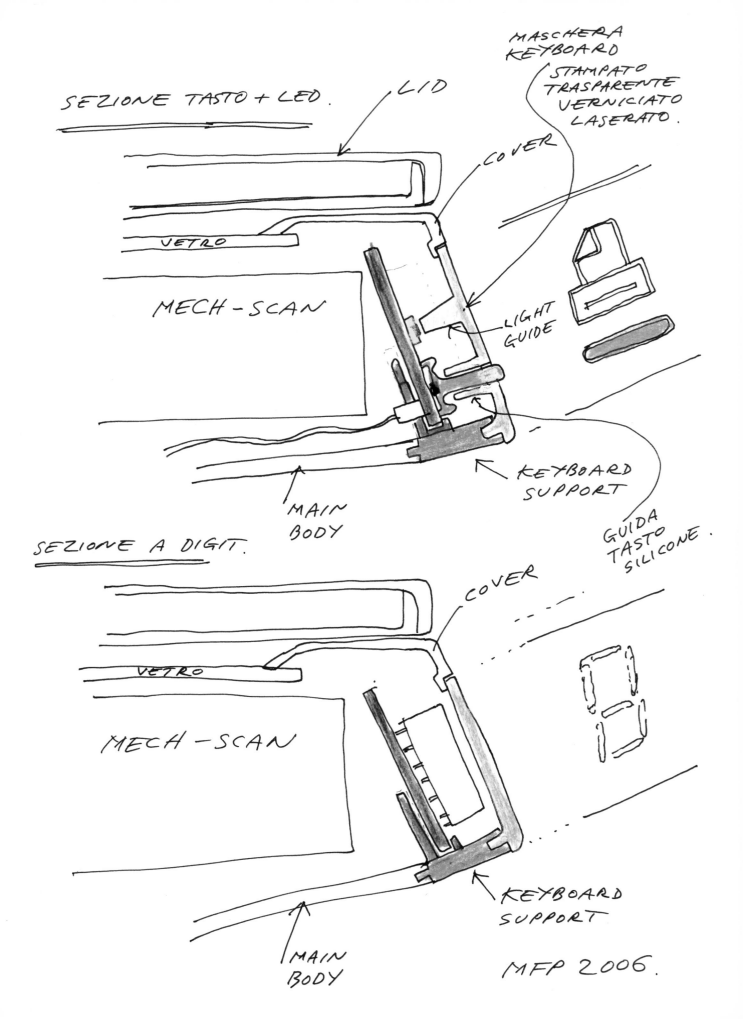

SEZIONE TASTO + LED.

LID

MASCHERA KEYBOARD

STAMPATO TRASPARENTE VERNICIATO LASERATO.

COVER

VETRO

MECH - SCAN

LIGHT GUIDE

KEYBOARD SUPPORT

MAIN BODY

SEZIONE A DIGIT.

GUIDA TASTO SILICONE.

COVER

VETRO

MECH - SCAN

KEYBOARD SUPPORT

MAIN BODY

MFP 2006.

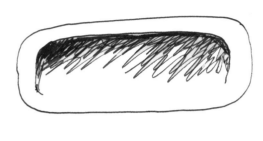

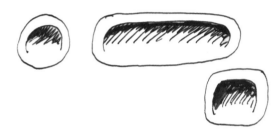

As an ex-student of James's from design college, I was familiar with his creative approach so I somehow knew what to expect. After browsing through Pamar's vast catalogue of handles, James's first, amusing reaction was: 'Is there anything possibly left to design?'

His design approach was typically distinctive and direct, expressed through three bold statements: 'Button' knobs as pure, corpulent forms, 'Smooth' flush handles as geometric and tactile shapes and 'Hole' handles built into the door panel where James cleverly gives the hole a perfect function! - Gordon Guillaumier

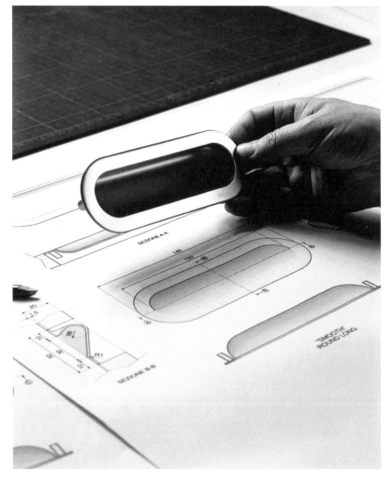

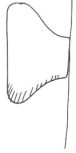

These days, we are surrounded by objects with
more or less clearly defined formats: A4 paper,
CDs, DVD cases... The constant proliferation
of these objects fills our lives with folders,
boxes and containers of every kind - there's
a real problem in organizing these objects in
daily life. Thousands of designs have attempted
to solve that problem. Box is a design that
takes account of the vast number of objects
we collect. - James Irvine

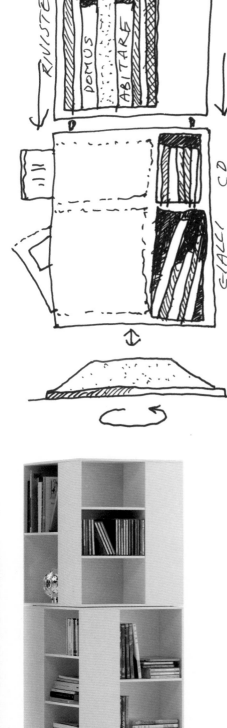

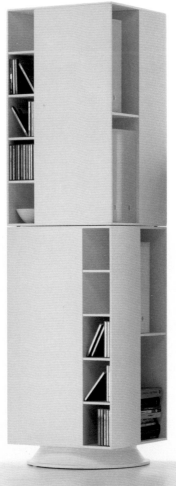

NAOTO FUKASAWA

SWEET
MODERNITY

James Irvine and Naoto Fukasawa at the Vitra booth,
Orgatec Cologne, 2010

FRANCESCA PICCHI: Naoto, you and James belong to the same
generation, and although you come from two very
different worlds you have had many similar experiences
– such as, for example, your formative time as product
designers for large electronics companies: in James's
case Olivetti and Toshiba, and in yours Seiko and
Epson. Can you tell the story of your friendship and
how you met?

NAOTO FUKASAWA: I got to know James through his designs.
I had associated his name with his work long before
I met him in person. I knew he was a partner of Sottsass
Associati, but the first product of his I admired was
the Piceno chair he had designed for Cappellini. It was
so delicate, so harmonious and so graceful, it had a
huge impact on me. At the time, I was a young designer,
unfamiliar with the leaders of European design.
I remember the design of the chair's legs, and overall
it had such a strong, definite character, it was almost
like a living thing. I believe that was the exact moment
when I began to know and admire James.

From then on his name remained imprinted in my
memory and, even though I hadn't met him in person,
I followed him through his projects and got closer
to him that way. There is a saying in Japanese that
translates roughly as: 'a person's name expresses that
person's nature'. I believe every object is in some way
a portrait of its designer, and when I first saw James's
chair I immediately thought it must have been designed
by a very friendly person. When, many years later,

I had an opportunity to meet him, my hunch was
confirmed: James was an extremely friendly person,
full of human warmth.

James was able to design incredibly complex
devices and perfectly produced objects. For me,
the Piceno chair is the piece that represents him
best because it reflects his humanity: it's as if it had
introduced him to me before we actually met.

FP: During the 1980s and 1990s your acquaintance
was indirect, you knew James essentially through his
reputation. Where were you during that time?

NF: In the late 1980s I was in the USA, where I worked
on electronic products modelled on Apple or other
industrial lines. Although I was fully immersed in that
industry, I was also intrigued by what was going on
in Europe and I followed closely the debate about
design that was developing in Italy. James was already
known as a young designer for Sottsass Associati. While
I was attracted by the debate about design in Europe,
at the same time I was very far away from it.

After starting out as a corporate designer in Japan
in the early 1980s, I had actually moved to California to
work for IDEO. Its founder, David Kelley, became
an important figure for me and my career. He had
a close relationship with the Italian design community
and he was very interested in the Italian scene. Later
on, James told me he had been in contact with David
because Sottsass Associati had developed some
projects with IDEO. So, even while working for a major
Silicon Valley design firm, I was dreaming of entering
that other world.

Some years later, when I felt the time had come
for me to return home, I told David Kelley that I wanted
to go back to Japan and to stop over in Europe en
route, to get to know the design scene better and
to meet its major players. That's how he gave me an
introduction to Ettore Sottsass, and I arrived in Milan
to meet him and other designers on the Milan scene.
I was beginning to find my feet in this milieu, to know
its big names and understand its various approaches.
In a sense I came into contact with a different way
of relating to the industry, and I realized that I wanted
to be part of it. But I had decided to return to Japan,
so I went back home.

FP: What conclusions did you draw about
European post-modern experiences, and the Italian
one in particular?

NF: As I see it, design encompasses two distinct elements: one is the idea, the other is the execution. Very often people believe a good designer is one who expresses good ideas, but I disagree. I believe execution is more important.

If we look at the work of Sottsass, one of the most significant exponents of the post-modern movement, we realize that in addition to designing expressive objects he was also able to design very well-executed products, such as the whole range he designed for Olivetti, or his cutlery for Alessi. He was a genius in everything he did, unlike other post-modern designers who lacked his deep understanding of the fundamentals of perfect execution.

As far as James is concerned, I think he felt he was slightly on the margins of the group of post-modern designers, perhaps simply because of his age, and felt the need to create his own personal network. In fact, he became part of the core of a group interested in searching for a new type of design, calmer, less 'flashy' – a group made up of friends who shared the idea of distancing themselves from post-modern design: first of all, Jasper Morrison, but also Konstantin Grcic, Thomas Sandell and Marc Newson – and many others who gravitated around Cappellini.

FP: In that connection, Jasper Morrison has often described how he almost accidentally found himself at the launch of Memphis in Milan in 1981, and how he had felt shocked but also intrigued because, although the whole thing was so different from what he knew, it nonetheless represented a totally novel and unexpected approach.

NF: Our generation, so to speak, was trying to distance itself from pure expression. We were more interested in the search for the essentials, which provided a common ground.

FP: Did James ever tell you about his experiences in Japan in the late 1980s, when he moved to Tokyo for a year as part of an exchange between Olivetti and Toshiba?

NF: When James spoke to me he always used the odd sentence in Japanese, and even though he wasn't fluent in my language those few words always made me feel at ease. In a way, we shared the experience of working as contract designers for a large company. He had worked for Toshiba: he'd been a 'salaryman', too.

He knew all about Japanese design and manufacturing; having worked in a large corporation, he also had a deep understanding of the stranger aspects of contemporary society's popular culture. His experience with Toshiba had enabled him to understand as an insider the typical conditions of a Japanese employee: a way of life which he seemed to have experienced with a certain curiosity. Unlike in Italy, where a designer is an independent professional, in Japan nearly ninety per cent of all designers work in-house, within a very rigid hierarchical structure. I think a European designer would find this rather strange, but I recall that James seemed rather amused by this system, where a designer is essentially a salaried employee.

FP: The contrast with the Italian situation must have been quite marked, since one of Sottsass's beliefs was that a designer must be independent vis-à-vis the industry. What he did was to establish consultancies with companies so that he could continue to bring his culture into the factory. He saw the designer as a kind of antenna, constantly in touch with social change. It was a completely new thing and he succeeded in making it the norm in Italian society. Later on, James, too, was a consultant for Olivetti, and even after joining Sottsass Associati he negotiated a way of continuing to work in his own studio at the same time.

NF: That experience expresses James's uniqueness. He was able to relate to leading designers like Sottsass, but also to move comfortably between the different levels of a company's hierarchy. He could establish excellent relationships with anyone at all.

FP: When did you meet in person?

NF: In the early 2000s, when Danese (a brand that was for me a kind of hero) made a comeback, I was struck again by James's design: he had designed pared-down objects of great character and in bright colours. In particular I remember a coat hanger and a shelf in extruded aluminium. I immediately felt I was looking at some amazing objects and a brand that had returned to its days of glory. Danese's is a story we all love, and it is inextricably linked with the work of Bruno Munari and Enzo Mari, two 'masters' I have always admired. When it was reborn, thanks to the work of a group of designers who revived the brand, James was part of that renewal. That's how I came across his name for the second time.

NAOTO FUKASAWA

At that time I had started to come into contact with European design culture. I met Jasper Morrison, with whom I became friends, and I began to work with European companies. It was at Danese that I finally met James. Although we had never met before, we were familiar with each other's work. An initial greeting and a few conversations were enough to forge a friendship. Since Jasper used to stay with James when he was in Milan, we would spend many evenings discussing design. Konstantin Grcic was often also with us. I gradually found myself part of that circle of designers of more or less the same generation, all of us sharing a similar attitude. It was the beginning of a new century. I think myself lucky to have been part of that group.

FP: So Milan was where you used to meet?

NF: James was at the centre of this hub and he was always up to date with what was happening. Every time I landed in Milan the first thing I did was phone James, who immediately rang other friends to organize a dinner: we'd meet round a table to discuss things, share ideas and news. It was the most normal thing in the world and it soon became a habit. I used to go to Milan every other month, and calling and seeing him became a ritual. James always knew everything about everyone; he was a great storyteller, his tales were entertaining, and after seeing him each time I knew all about the changes and developments in the design world. He was very amusing.

So when, later on, I became more involved in the Muji project, it was completely natural for me to invite James to design the new Muji products, with Jasper Morrison, Konstantin Grcic and Sam Hecht, whom I'd met at IDEO. This new venture was called 'World designers'. We needed someone who could maintain contact with Japan and the people at Muji, and we immediately thought of James as the right person to keep the lines of communication open. James was not only a very friendly person but he had the added virtue of speaking a bit of Japanese. In addition to that, he understood Japanese culture and knew how best to approach people. Generally speaking, Japanese people are reserved, and he was the right person to break the ice.

At that time James was focusing on his work for Thonet. The Loop chair he designed for Thonet joined the Piceno and his designs for Danese, all of them enhancing his reputation. And meanwhile, our friendship was becoming stronger.

FP: Muji's identity is based on being 'non-branded'; the 'World designers' venture, by involving well-known designers, marks a change. What was it that changed?

NF: The word 'Muji' actually means 'no design'. That means that working with designers wasn't in its brief. But given the increase in its range of products, it became necessary to involve designers, so as to design things differently and make the products simpler and more accessible. It was in that altered culture that my design for a wall-mounted CD player took shape: I had developed it independently, and Muji decided to put it into production. This object turned out to be one of the key elements in that change, because it showed how the no-design idea could be combined with the work of a designer.

FP: Am I right in saying that with the 'World designers' experience, Muji introduced for the first time to Japan a new type of open relationship between designer and industry?

NF: As I said, Muji had never had a specific relationship with any designer. It has a design advisory board, to which I and others, including Kenya Hara, belong. 'World designers' was therefore the first design team called upon to work for Muji. Since the brand, like the range of products, was growing fast, I persuaded the board that only a design team could manage this increasing complexity.

It was then that Masaaki Kanai, Muji's president, decided to establish an international design department, since Muji could no longer see itself as an exclusively Japanese brand and needed both the experiences and the opinions of others. The 'World designers' group of designers was born in that context. It included Jasper Morrison, Konstantin Grcic, Sam Hecht and myself (I also sat on the design advisory board). James had the role of 'commander in chief', or something like that.

FP: Muji's image is associated with the idea of anonymous design. How could a group of designers with such strong identities fit into that concept? Were there specific requests to define a common language?

NF: Enzo Mari once said he'd always been a Muji designer, long before Muji actually existed. There are many examples of good design that have their

MUJI×THONETの未来
家具の次なるスタンダードは、今、ここから生まれる。

曲木椅子の原型「No.14」と、バウハウスで考案されたスチールパイプの家具。
このモダンデザインの名作が生まれた当時の理念に立ち返って、
無印良品が完成させた「MUJI manufactured by THONET」を紹介しよう。

Photos ATSUSHI NAKAMICHI (P.198~199 Nacása & Partners Inc.) MASAO MURABAYASHI (portrait)
Text TAKAHIRO TSUCHIDA

2008 MUJI No.14

無印良品とトーネットの
奇跡的なコラボレーション

ここで紹介する無印良品の家具には、ルーツがある。背もたれから後脚への曲線が美しい「MUJI No.14」は、1859年にミヒャエル・トーネットが発表した曲木椅子「No.14」のリデザイン。凛としてモダンな「MUJI スチールパイプチェア＆デスク」は、1920年代にバウハウスで生まれたスチールパイプ製の家具のリデザインだ。

トーネットの曲木椅子やバウハウスのスチールパイプの家具は、共に時代を超えた名作と評される。双方に共通するのは、多くの人々が使える優れた家具を追求して生まれたデザインだということ。「No.14」は、蒸気を使った曲木技術を応用し、美しさと低価格を実現したものだ。またバウハウスのデザイナーが完成させたスチールパイプの家具は、当時は工業素材でしかなかったパイプに、近代化する生活にふさわしいフォルムと機能を与えた。

これらの家具はいずれも、ドイツの名門家具メーカーであるトーネット社が作り続けている。ただし現在は、どちらも日用品としてはあまりに高価なものになってしまった。それがデザインの価値と品質を反映しているとしても、デザイナーの本来の意図からは大きな隔たりがあるはずだ。

「MUJI manufactured by THONET」の第1弾として発表された「MUJI No.14」と「MUJI スチールパイプチェア＆デスク」は、そんな矛盾に対する無印良品からの解答だ。オリジナルのデザインを合理的に進化させ、製作工程を見直して、当初の理念を現代に蘇らせようとしたのだ。リデザインは、ジェームス・アーヴァインが「MUJI

beginnings in the idea of anonymous design: think of the work of Achille Castiglioni for instance. The same attitude can be seen in Jasper Morrison, Konstantin Grcic or in James himself. In short, Muji invited people who were outside a post-modern stylistic approach, inspired by an emotional vision of design.

The designers chosen by Muji were not interested in selling their own names through the products, but wanted to go down a route inspired by a certain kind of simplicity, typical of anonymous design. That's the way it was: Muji asked us to design some products and we agreed.

FP: Can you say a bit more about James's role?

NF: James had a key role within Muji in terms of communication, design and production. At one point Muji's president became interested in establishing relationships with producers of iconic designs, such as Thonet. He was particularly interested in the bentwood Chair No. 14, in beech, which he believed was a perfect design – ideal for Muji. James, as Thonet's art director, became the link and established contact. Thonet agreed to supply the Chair No. 14 as long as we made some modifications.

On the whole, none of the designers in the 'World designers' group was really convinced that the Chair No. 14 was right for Muji, and in any case no one felt able to face redesigning an iconic piece of that kind, so we all turned to James and said 'Hey, this is a job for you.'

James took on the project and approached the redesign of Thonet's Chair No. 14 with the utmost respect, while also trying to deviate slightly from the original model: the result was an object with strong iconic features. In this case, as in a number of others, when dealing with a piece of design history James was able to introduce elements of great naturalness and elegance. It was his signature: to design products that were professional while also intuitive and user-friendly.

FP: When faced with an iconic design like the bentwood chair, it's as if he performed a conjuring trick: with his sleight of hand he made the chair disappear by camouflaging it in juxtaposition with the table. It is a feature that is both playful and elegant, within a very serious project.

NF: That was his way of de-dramatizing function. He had a functionalist approach that was nevertheless full of irony and humour. The back of the chair was the hardest part to resolve. His earliest designs included a mesh back, and later, after a lot of experimentation, he arrived at this solution, which stunned everybody.

FP: Looking at his designs I was struck by the way he always looked for the soul in an object, as if, even within the extreme abstraction of the visual language, he was looking at an object as a kind of character, to be brought to life.

NF: That's exactly what struck me ever since that first chair design for Cappellini: he always tried to design objects as if they were human beings or animals. It was one of his typical traits, this friendly, intuitive nature: to design objects with a friendly expression.

FP: Having been privileged to leaf through his sketchbooks, I can say they are full of tiny details that point to a suggestion that objects have a personality inside them. His sketches are full of faces or other human features, which he has tried to transfer into objects, even if by using very abstract lines. Many sketches exist, for instance, for the Muji desk fan: they all show great care in designing the small knob for regulating airflow, because he was trying to incorporate a smile. I think that encapsulates his idea of design: his products are looking for the smile within a person.

After Thonet and Muji, it was the turn of Marsotto: another important episode in James's story.

NF: As I said, he had the role of a hub, or centre, for the community of designer friends, and not only at Muji. To involve friends in his projects was part of his nature: he loved working in a group. So when he became art director at Marsotto it was wholly natural for him to involve his network of friends and designers in developing the project: he had the knack of picking the right people to make things happen. And I was very fortunate to have been invited to be part of this group.

FP: Marble is a material with a very solid tradition. In Italy it is quite usual to go to a quarry and choose a piece to work on, in exactly the same way as Michelangelo did in the sixteenth century. As a company, Marsotto specializes in working in marble: were you already familiar with this material?

NF: It was the first time I had had to deal with marble, but James's presence and that of the others made it perfectly easy for me. James never formulated a precise request, but in the very instant he asked us to design something we all knew that the outcome would be interesting. It's the kind of collaboration that I have no hesitation in calling a 'jam session'. James, in particular, had this way of working with others by putting them at ease: we were comfortable working together, like musicians who meet up to improvise with no prearranged plan – on the contrary, improvising on a scheme of familiar chords and themes. That's how we worked. It all happened very easily, as though the project had been there waiting for us.

Work meetings were also an opportunity to meet and a chance for each of us to test our own ability through dialogue with the others. These meetings were a fertile ground for the exchange of ideas, and they could be said to have been an integral part of the design process. It was a very pleasant way of working.

FP: This idea of the collective is interesting because I think that sharing his work – which was also his pleasure – with a group of friends was part of James's vision of design.

You have often shared the idea of working together, if not as a design movement, certainly as a very cohesive group. Suffice it to mention the Super Normal experience that you shared with Jasper Morrison, or the work for Muji, or again the experience at Marsotto, where James brought you all together. You say James performed the role of hub. How would you describe that position?

NF: James wasn't exactly a philospher – more the kind of person who loved design with the same passion as he loved motorbikes. That's the person he was. When I see his studio, the objects he surrounded himself with, his collections, the things he liked, I understand the influence they had on his way of designing, because they were part of his way of seeing design. He was like a child who enjoys drawing things.

Because he loved design so much, James also loved talking about it; he liked to know what others thought. Had he been a philosopher, people might have experienced him as distant; instead, he was easy to talk to. There was an immediate feeling of friendship. He was warm and also very generous in relation to design. That's why he was able to build a network of that kind: everyone loved him. As I said, James was the hub of

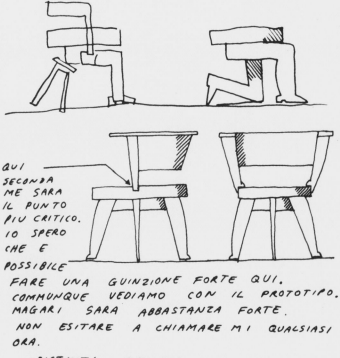

QUI SECONDA ME SARA IL PUNTO PIU CRITICO. IO SPERO CHE E POSSIBILE FARE UNA GUINZIONE FORTE QUI. COMMUNQUE VEDIAMO CON IL PROTOTIPO. MAGARI SARA ABBASTANZA FORTE. NON ESITARE A CHIAMARE MI QUALSIASI ORA.

DISTINTI SALUTI

Sketches for the Piceno chair, early 1990s

a circle of people whose approach was totally new, very different from what had been happening before. His loss is felt very keenly. This feeling of loss is even more powerful when I come to Milan. And I think this is true for the others, too.

FP: How would you describe the bond that united your group of people who were fundamentally heterogeneous, and had strong individual identities?

NF: I can't define it as a formal design movement, more as a group of friends who met and worked together. Being part of this community has been important for me, as both an individual and a designer. James, in particular, has been a very important presence, since, like all Japanese people, I'm reserved, and James, on the contrary, was warm, friendly and also very modest.

I remember that once, talking about Jasper and myself, he said, 'You two work really hard thinking about design, while I'm a simple fellow who just enjoys designing, that's my way.' Perhaps he didn't use those exact words, but that's what he meant.

He didn't like it when the designer's ego had the upper hand. But he did have a strong personality that set him apart from everyone else.

ALBERTO MEDA

THE
ECOLOGY
OF
QUALITY

Studio Irvine, 2005 (L-R: Davide Mariani, Maddalena Casadei, Dunja Weber, Cristina Massocchi, James Irvine)

Our friendship goes back to the year 2000 when we were both invited by Arabia – a pioneering brand in Scandinavian design – to take part in a workshop focusing on designing highly innovative ceramic products. When James and I left on the trip we hardly knew each other, but we felt an immediate liking for one another. I was struck by his open, inquisitive nature, and his humanity – that of someone who is genuinely friendly and loves meeting and getting to know people. I was interested in environmental issues and designed a carafe that would encourage the drinking of tap water, thus reducing the use of plastic bottles. I remember that James designed a very elegant set for growing lettuce and putting it straight on the table. Our designs received a moderately positive response from the public, but never developed beyond the prototype stage.

After Arabia, we would happen to bump into each other from time to time at Frankfurt airport. At that time James was doing a huge amount of travelling, because he was teaching at Karlsruhe and also went frequently to Hanover for the city bus project he was working on, which kept him constantly on the move: he was like an ambassador for Lufthansa. I travelled much less, but still moved about quite a bit, and so, without arranging it, we would happen to meet at the airport: it was a pleasant opportunity to have a beer and chat about the world of design while waiting for our connecting flights.

Our most important collaboration was definitely the project for Olivetti, which we developed together and to which we put both our names. We happened to meet one evening at some do, and discovered that both of us had been sent a proposal for a new design project by Olivetti. Since we were good friends, we immediately started gossiping, and sharing our ideas. Then, almost for fun, we said: 'Supposing we did it together?' And that's what we did. Let's surprise them all! And it was great fun, instructive and stimulating. For James, too, I think. That proposal, which started almost as a joke, was enthusiastically accepted by Olivetti's management, and they decided to award us the project. That was the beginning of a three-year-long adventure; we worked for Olivetti from 2004 to 2007.

During that time I learned to appreciate James's 'English' way of doing things: precise and organized, with a strong experimental and empirical bent. I liked the easy-going atmosphere in his studio, where nobody had any secrets. It was all very direct and transparent, with none of the hypocrisy that often plagues Italian studios. My studio wasn't organized like James's, where there were three assistants and a workshop where they made polystyrene models. That's why I almost always went there to work, and that way I discovered his ability to handle not just his pencil but his relationships with his colleagues, and the complexity of running a small firm. The fish restaurant behind his studio, where he was very much at home, was a place where we could relax and talk a lot of nonsense, like two kids. They are very happy memories for me.

Apart from these pleasant interludes, we worked hard. James had a deep understanding of the field of product design, a professionalism that I believe has not been fully recognized; my contribution was my engineering background. It worked well. The scope of our collaboration with Olivetti was wider than the range of products that actually became

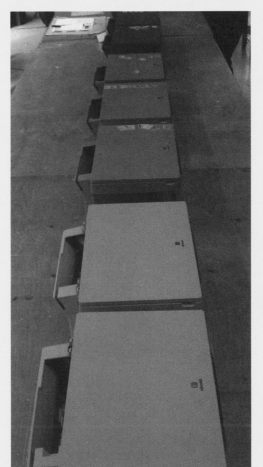

L: Sequence of prototypes for Simple Way multi-function printer for Olivetti, designed by Irvine and Meda, 2005
R: Irvine and Meda in the Viale Piceno studio, 2005

available on the market. In addition to the two MFP (multi-function printer) models, the Any Way and the Simple Way, we also designed a special model intended for use in banks (the PR2) and one for the postal service (the PR6), plus a fax machine, which never went into production.

In 2005, James put my name forward for the Honorary Royal Designer for Industry award, and at the ceremony in London I had the opportunity to meet his father, a fine architect who had worked for Olivetti in the glory days. I then understood more clearly the affection James felt towards Olivetti and his disappointment, which I shared, at the failure of our printer project, when the machine was discontinued after a very short time, and the new owners showed no interest in reviving the Olivetti brand. When we met and first thought about sharing the project for Olivetti, I didn't realize that James had so strong an emotional investment in it, similar to how I felt about Kartell, where I had started off as a designer and towards which I still feel a certain attachment.

But when I met his father and we chatted about the history of their ties with Olivetti, it transpired that James's first commission had been for Olivetti, where he met Ettore Sottsass and Michele De Lucchi, and that thanks to Olivetti he had spent a year in Tokyo, working for Toshiba. In short, I realized that, what with his father's connection and his own early career, James's motivation for the project – and therefore I guess his disappointment – had been stronger than mine. I can now say that the MFP story ended badly due to the ineptitude of the management, who didn't know how to launch the new printer in a 'protected' way, rather than immediately exposing it to direct competition with leading global brands in the distribution networks (even Apple had started by creating separate distribution systems for its own products). But the worst mistake was their inability to organize the supply of ink cartridges, which proved very difficult to source. And to think that the idea of the printer came about precisely to exploit the capacity for producing cartridges at Olivetti's factory at Arnad!

At the time, that factory, up in the mountains in the Val d'Aosta, was the last remaining place in Europe able to carry out the entire technical process of making silicon for printer-heads, the core of ink-jet printing. The whole production cycle required working environments with a modified atmosphere, and the contrast between the mountain landscape outside, and the controlled conditions inside, with workers wearing protective clothing, was striking. In short, all this had justified our hope that it would be possible to restore the brand to its former eminence.

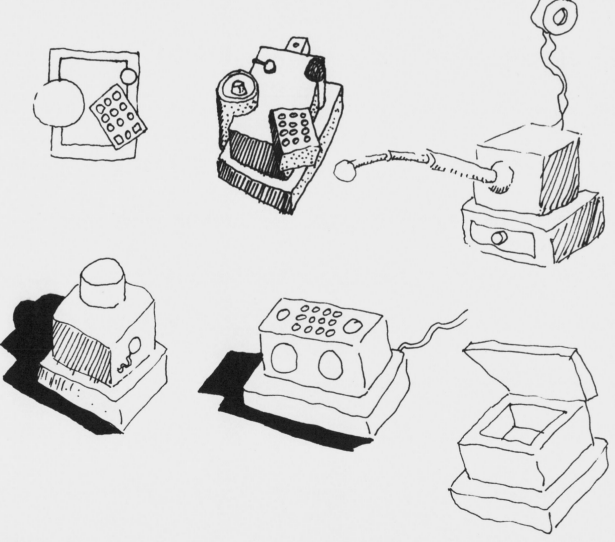

Prototypes for telephone for LG, 2007

Prototype for an unrealized bus shelter for Stroer, 2001

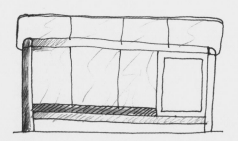

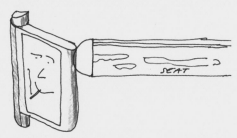

Sketches for an unrealized bus shelter for Stroer, 2001

In a way, the Olivetti story affected us more than we realized. It led us naturally towards a certain formal rigour and spareness, but above all it was a spur towards elegance. Essentially, the approach to the design of that new generation of multi-function printers using ink-jet technology was based on simplifying their shape and their use. The idea was that devices of this kind, first intended for the office and then adopted for home use, should have the clearest and simplest architecture possible. The request to design a multifunctional object offered a degree of freedom in the arrangement of its internal components, and enabled us to reach a new solution for the position of the head, making it accessible from the top by opening the device like a book. The arrangement of the user interface, on the front and easy to reach, was also in keeping with the overall design and the clarity of its architecture.

It was very interesting for me to engage in a working dialogue with James. Whenever we had to formulate an idea or think of a new solution, we would discuss it, in words or doodles, then we would do our 'homework', and pass it on to the other, as a way of moving the project forwards in this joint fashion. We have countless drawings that show our constant exchange of ideas, and our way of dialoguing through drawings. James had a pragmatic approach; he had that way of thinking with his hands, in a direct way, by making prototypes. You can't imagine how many 'catwalk' displays we did with our small models.

I recall that at the time when we began to discuss the project for Olivetti, 1980-style abstruse forms were everywhere, which I could only describe as 'loaf-shaped'. Computers had reintroduced rounded forms that were without character but arrogantly proclaimed their own presence. With the Olivetti management we decided on a series of keywords, such as 'iconic simplicity' and 'elegance of technology'. That was our common ground: to define ourselves by simplicity and to design a form people could live with comfortably at home.

We very much liked the idea that the machine was not monolithic, that it should demonstrate a kind of honesty in its construction, and that its volume should therefore be built round the organization of its internal components. We both liked the idea of trying to articulate the architecture of the machine in a better way. In short, we had fun working, and almost without noticing it we succeeded in making hundreds of models and exploring a wide variety of solutions. As far as Olivetti was concerned, we felt a need to re-engage a positive energy, and that ours was a project with psychological and human dimensions, and in that sense I believe we succeeded.

After the printer project we continued to see each other quite often and took a few holidays together in Tuscany. James's ability to be at the place where interesting people, cultures and worlds coincided was of inestimable value. Today I miss him greatly.

THOMAS SANDELL

MODERN CLASSICS WITH A SIMPLE TWIST

FRANCESCA PICCHI: Can you help us trace the story of your relationship with James?

THOMAS SANDELL: James and I met through Jasper Morrison. They were organizing Progetto Oggetto for Cappellini and invited me to join the project. I flew out to Milan where I met James for the first time and we soon became friends. James and Jasper had brought together around twenty designers from all over the world – James was the only one who lived in Milan, spoke the language and knew his way around. He was part of the city itself, and in a way the whole project centred round him; he was a key person for all the designers.

FP: I'm trying to identify what you all had in common. What do you think it was?

TS: Despite our different backgrounds, we shared a common search for a kind of new, classic contemporary design after the excess of self-expression in the 1980s.

FP: How would you describe his design approach?

TS: James's approach to design can be seen as a kind of mixture: what we could call Scandinavian modernism was dominant, but with an Italian twist. That link with the cultural environment he found in Milan is clearly visible in his work. For example, I remember a collection of glass vases, in which that influence is especially clear, and also his design for a lamp in the shape of a pig that I like very much and which James designed right at the beginning of his career. It's a design I know well, because I don't believe many examples were made, and I'm lucky enough to own one of them. I think the reason I've always liked it is that I can see in it the kind of irony that I admired so much in James. It's an object that really expresses his 'Pop' side, his typically British sense of humour. There's this subtle irony in everything James made that I've always really appreciated: the freedom to introduce that bit of added value, a smile.

FP: But what brought you together, surely, was your interest in the modern design idiom.

TS: To begin with, yes. It was the reason we met and that led me to take part in a project like Progetto Oggetto. During the development and presentation of the project we had time to hang out together. Every time I arrived in Milan the first thing I did, as soon as I got off the plane, was call him and arrange to meet. Over the years we became ever closer friends, and when an opportunity arose for working on a project for Ikea I thought of collaborating with James. A few years previously I had been responsible with Thomas Eriksson for the art direction of Ikea's design collection, PS Collection, presented in Milan in 1995. Our collaboration continued and a few years later I was asked to think about a new project, using rattan in products to be manufactured in China. It was then that I called James. We didn't just go to visit the factories in a remote part of central China, but we also stopped in Hong Kong and Macao. It was my first visit to China and I think it was for him too. It was great fun. When I went there again recently I found it all completely different: where there had been open country there were now motorways and high-speed railways.

FP: What did you have in common from the point of view of design?

TS: Despite everything, I would say it was the search for a kind of modern classicism based on a pared-down idiom and simple forms, one whose roots were in modernist thinking, but interpreted in a contemporary key. While it was not exactly a topic of discussion, it was an idea we shared, an area of common ground. We shared not only a way of looking at design but also the fact that we liked the same things and shared a frame of reference.

FP: James had a special connection with Scandinavia, Sweden in particular. His first one-man exhibition was held in Stockholm and he always retained close links with Swedish companies like CBI, Asplund, Swedese and Wästberg. What do you think that link with Scandinavian design consisted of?

TS: In the Scandinavian tradition it's very natural to design simple everyday objects. If you think about it, the same idea was the basis for Cappellini's Progetto Oggetto: something that was well designed, but didn't need to shout out loud. If we see it in proper perspective, it was something new, almost transgressive. Having said that, James loved Scandinavian design and he also had a deep knowledge of its history. I recall that he had a particular passion for the work of Bruno Mathsson,

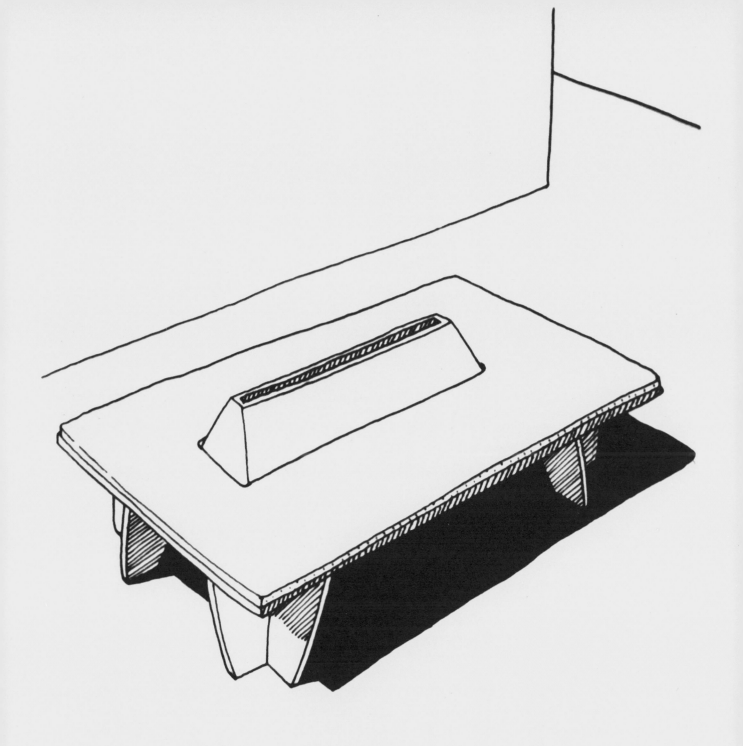

"BENCH"
FOR
UPPSALA CASTLE

JAMES IRVINE
1994

Sketch for a bench, 1994

THOMAS SANDELL

Irvine and the Gunghult rattan chair for Ikea, 2002

Irvine and Thomas Sandell at the Marsotto premises in Bovolone, choosing marble for Sandell's House of Marble, 2010

a designer who helped create the legend of the 'Scandinavian modern'. Mathsson was self-taught, his family were furniture-makers and he approached modernism in a way that was entirely instinctive. He was one of the first people, with Alvar Aalto, to experiment with curved laminate, and achieved a degree of refined detail while also stressing the material's resistance. James had been acquainted with Mathsson since he was a child, and his famous armchair in plaited webbing – a classic found in the collection at MoMA – formed part of his childhood landscape. He loved him so much that he used the table-leg that Mathsson had designed with a mathematician friend to furnish his studio. When he was invited to design for Swedese Möbler, a classic Swedish furniture factory founded after the war by Yngve Ekström, a designer of Mathsson's generation, it was an opportunity for James to engage with that tradition, and in fact he designed a chair in curved beech that could have been the work of a Swedish designer; it's an elegant chair, beautifully designed.

Something James was very adept at was getting on good terms with manufacturers, in the sense that when he was asked to do a project for a company, he put a great effort into understanding its essence: its history, its technical capability and its desired position in the market. He paid great attention to that aspect, which could be called each factory's 'character'. Another thing that really struck me about his approach to his work was the fact that he was highly organized. He had developed a system of folders in which he filed all his material relating to a project, which he then bound in book form. Everything was there: his preliminary sketches, all the documents and correspondence, technical reports, load tests, exchanges of opinion with the manufacturer and the marketing people, all the drawings and rejected solutions. Every project was described in those black books. Every time I went to see him in his studio I was fascinated. I should also add that James's studio, or rather, the studios he had in Milan over the years, and especially the last one, were all beautiful, welcoming places, where you could see his personal touch. Where everything was 'very James'.

FP: It's curious that everyone should use that phrase to describe the special nature of James's work. How would you explain it?

TS: I could only describe it as something that was in keeping with his character. James was always cheerful, always entertaining and ironic, and he was also very generous. I'm an architect and I do a lot of work in the field of architecture, but I have to say the world of design is very welcoming, in the sense that designers tend to share a lot of things and invite each other to collaborate. If you think about it, Progetto Oggetto, B&B Italia and Marsotto were all group projects that came about because of the pleasure people took in working together, in which James played a central part.

Take the case of B&B for example: when he invited me to take part in a collection he was organizing for them, James had been contacted by the company because they were interested in finding new blood. They had asked James to start researching furniture for the young generation, and he said he didn't feel able to carry out the project on his own and he had suggested involving Marc Newson and me. Our group held many meetings, trying to invent new types of furniture, studying current changes in home-living and consumption patterns. We worked in close contact with the company's research and development division, an incredible set-up with expert craftsmen, and in the end we put into production a series of pieces of furniture presented at the Salone del Mobile in 1998. James designed the Radar armchair, Marc a table that was held together by a special steel cable, and I designed a table with a depression in the middle of the Corian tabletop that acted as a receptacle and centrepiece.

Then there was Marsotto, a very good example. They managed to put together an extraordinary group of designers thanks only to James's personal qualities. Marsotto is very small, and I believe no other company in the world could boast of having designers of comparable calibre working for them. It's truly a piece of design history. It's a fantastic collection, entirely due to James's ability to relate to people, his charm and personality. And I was very happy to be part of the project, if only because I believe I designed my best pieces for it.

Murano bowls for Conde Nast, 2002

Out in the open. Soaking up the sun. Brioche with
a cappuccino. Reading the paper. French bread and
cheese. A fiasco of Chianti. Olives and salami. Someone
dives in the pool. In the shade of a tree. Laughter
on the terrace. Lunch for eight. Aperitivo for two.
Life is not so bad after all... Out in the open with
Open. - James Irvine

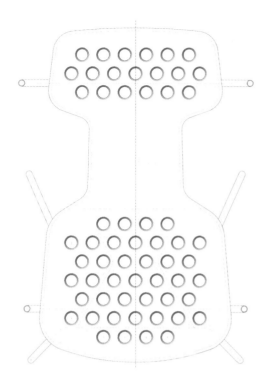

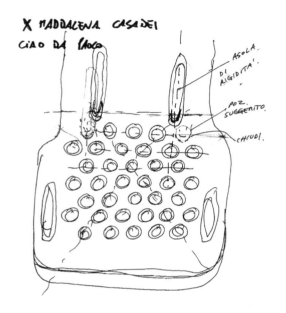

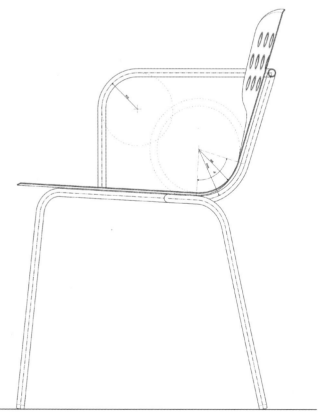

This three-legged wooden table was
designed to be completly collapsible
so as to be easily delivered by mail

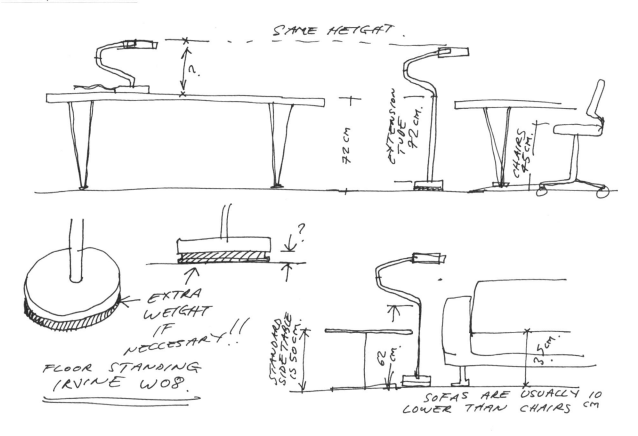

SAME HEIGHT.

72 CM

EXTENSION TUBE 72 CM.

CHAIRS 45 CM.

EXTRA WEIGHT IF NECCESARY!!

FLOOR STANDING IRVINE W08.

STANDARD SIDE TABLE IS 50 CM.

62 CM

35 CM.

SOFAS ARE USUALLY 10 CM LOWER THAN CHAIRS

The task lamp is one of those design projects which
always has to measure itself with great masterpieces
from the past. Hundreds have been invented over the
years. Some of them so brilliant that they are hard
to beat. They are full of springs and knobs and
complicated hinges. Sure, you can design another one
of these but my feeling is that perhaps there is the
space for a simplified mechanism. An object which is
calm. It does move, but does not do everything. For me
that's enough and maybe for some other people too.
- James Irvine

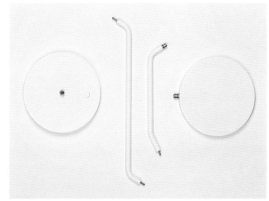

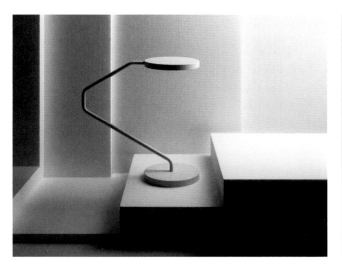

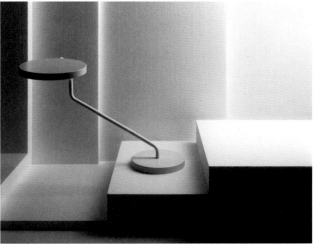

As with all designs involving craftsmanship, James felt free to express himself with irony and spontaneity. This design reflects his close connection with Italy and with the Italians and our habits. It's a tribute - an expression of love for speed and for typically Italian vehicles, especially those found in Sardinia: bicycles, scooters, the Ape three-wheeled van, the Fiat 500 and the Panda... plus one that sneaked in - James's BSA motorbike!
- Maddalena Casadei

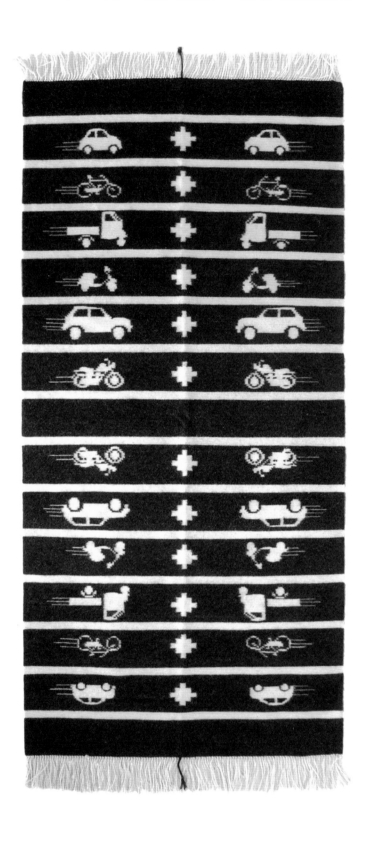

1. FACE PUZZLE (2008)

It's nice when things aren't too explicit; that's when they can make the strongest statement. The name Muji means 'no-brand', yet it is one of the strongest brands. The apparently simple design of this children's toy - when you rotate the eyes, nose and mouth the expression changes - is only one example of the way this Japanese company supports craftsmanship. - James Irvine

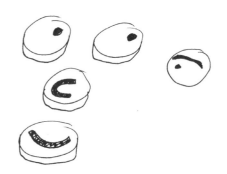
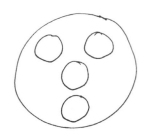

2. DESK FAN (2012)

Desk Fan meets the energy-saving requirements that are all the more stringent in post-earthquake Japan, complying with the country's national plan for energy conservation. When the small fan is used at the work-station itself, it reduces the need for air conditioning, saving energy. Desk Fan is powered directly from the computer, via a USB port. It consists of two fans that work together, creating a vortex effect, enhancing the power of the device, despite its small size. - James Irvine

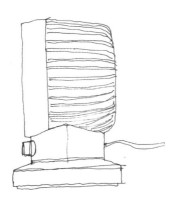

3. ALUMINIUM PEN CASE (2013)

We carefully studied the existing design of the Muji aluminium pen case: we looked at the manufacturing process and tried to respect all the processes as much as possible. Our proposal is for a design using two identical shells. In this way, the circular form of the edges is complete, both back and front. The existing Muji design has a square back where the hinge is located. The clip - or rather clips - on our design, work like a lady's purse. The case is opened using both thumbs. Because both identical shells of the design are curved, the pen case is more rigid. - James Irvine

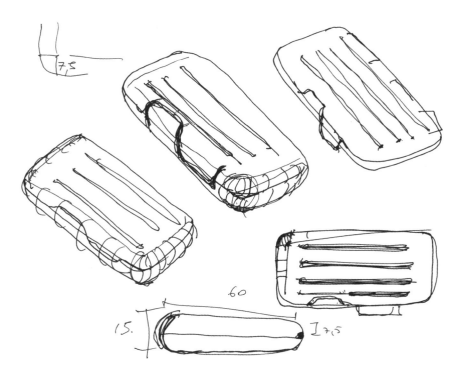

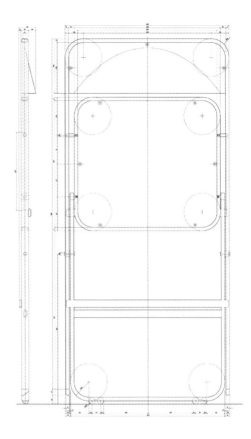

4. FOLDING CHAIR (2013)

James was very familiar with the idea of the folding chair, and the difficulties involved in designing something that had to be completely flat. He was equally familiar with the small size of Japanese houses, and he therefore imagined a chair which, when folded, would fill the same space as its profile. He wanted to create a super-flat chair: as light and unobtrusive as possible. Hence the choice of extruded aluminium with a plastic back and seat. - Maddalena Casadei

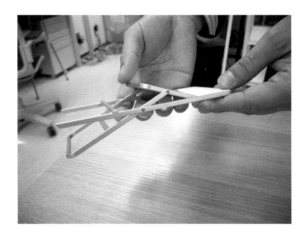

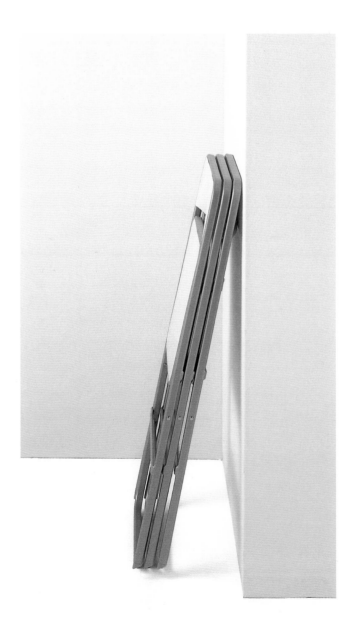

5. ULTRA LIGHT CHAIR (2013)

This project pays homage to a wooden chair
that has been produced in Chiavari, Italy
for the last 150 years: a chair that even
today still passes the strict modern safety
tests. It is such a great construction
concept. We designed it to be more modern,
and above all more Muji. We also conceived
a detachable, washable fabric seat instead
of the original expensive Indian cane
version. - James Irvine

One of the best things that can happen to a designer is the opportunity to work with a company that has a history and a context. I worked with the fifth generation of the Thonet family, and we had a most interesting relationship. Their Chair No. 14 - the iconic bentwood chair which has been in production since 1859 - had become something of an artwork, far removed from its mass-market origins. As soon as Masaaki Kanai, CEO of Muji, recognized much of Muji's ethos and philosophy in the No. 14 design, he asked me to revisit it: a highly dangerous undertaking that just so happened to turn out well. To take on the challenge of the Thonet No. 14 was the height of arrogance, as Stephen Bayley wrote provocatively in the *Guardian*: 'The job of adapting a classic designed for Vienna café society to the needs of the Twitter era meant a flirtation with hubris for James Irvine.'

I was already creative director at Thonet, and a consultant for Muji, and in 2007 I put the two companies in contact, with the idea of repositioning the German brand, which was still producing the chair in Frankenberg, at high cost. In particular, the Muji / Thonet Chair No. 14 design achieved the goal of 'making it easier for people between the ages of 18 and 35 to relate to the Thonet brand,' set by Roland Ohnacker, the managing director.

The only thing that remains unchanged in the new chair, compared with the original, is the single curve forming the back legs and the chair-back. On the back, the second bentwood hoop has been replaced by a much less costly horizontal slat, so that when the chair is at the table, it becomes literally invisible. - James Irvine

No.1
トーネット・チェア第一号。背部
分の優美な曲線は積層合板の技術の極みと言える。

No.4
後脚と背当ては積層合板、
その他は無垢材で製作。
トーネット初の量産家具。

No.14
無垢材の曲木のみで製作。
マスプロダクションの原形ともいわれる、トーネットの代名詞。

No.18
北米向け輸出用に開発した、
1㎡に36脚分の部品が収まる運搬効率の良い組立式。

No.56
他社の類似品に対抗するため端材を無駄なく使用し、
価格を低廉にしたモデル。

MUJI
「多くの人に良質の椅子を」というミヒャエル・トーネットの理念のもと、
嗜好品ではなく、すぐそばで当たり前に使える家具として新たに開発した。

Participating designers:

JAMES IRVINE
JASPER MORRISON
KONSTANTIN GRCIC
MADDALENA CASADEI
NAOTO FUKASAWA
THOMAS SANDELL
ALBERTO MEDA
CLAESSON KOIVISTO RUNE
JOEL BERG
ROSS LOVEGROVE
DAVID CHIPPERFIELD

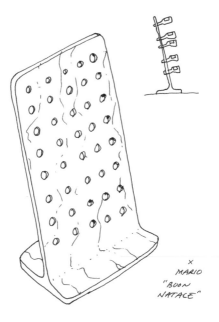

x
MARIO
"BUON
NATALE"

IRVINE

My first meeting with Mario and Costanza Marsotto was one of those happy meetings where we almost immediately found that we enjoyed working together. I was put in touch with them to do a project for the Marmomacc fair in Verona, Italy - the biggest and most important marble and stone fair in the world. It was a new environment for me. Incredibly exciting but at the same time rather daunting. Marble, the material of the Romans and Greeks. The most noble of materials.

Italy is full of the most extraordinary small companies with extraordinary skills. Marsotto like many others, is a company that has been waiting for their chance to glow - to test themselves. Following our first project together, a series of circular discs on columns, we understood that there were fantastic possibilities. Marble, in a sense a forgotten material, has been rediscovered over the past few years. Some extraordinary pieces have been realized. However they have always remained rather exclusive. As if marble is a material which is only for floors or masterpieces. Marble is in fact a rather normal material in Italy. Why not try to do some accessible products, we asked ourselves? Above all why not try to do pieces which are totally in marble? Not just the top of a table, or a chunky ashtray.

Together we arrived at the idea of Marsotto Edizioni. A place to create products... a place for designers to realize their ideas. I knew that I had to call people who would be in tune with this idea to do real things, or at least this was the intention.

Together we have created almost 30 products. The designers are a mix of nationalities. German, English, Swedish, Japanese and Italian. The products created in white Carrara marble are made using CNC machinery and finished by hand. What many people don't know is that the marble from Carrara is 190,000,000 years old. Yes one hundred and ninety million years old. It is estimated that there are 60,000,000,000 cubic metres of marble in the mountains of Carrara. Put more simply that is 60 cubic kilometeres. A lot of material hidden away and just waiting to be made into useful, and maybe not useful, things. - James Irvine

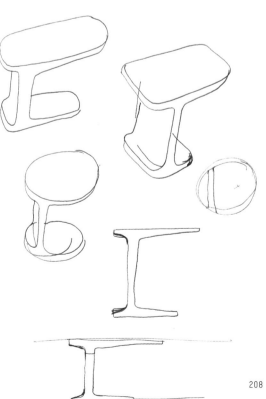

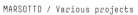

MARSOTTO / Various projects

It is commonly expected that famous designers apply their distinctive formal signature to their new designs so that their products become easily recognizable and visually jump out. For the project of Mellow Light, the redesign of an already hugely successful product range by the leading lighting company Zumtobel, just the opposite is true. Huge amounts of effort were spent in making the luminaire and its details 'invisible'.

With its distinct bevel feature, the luminaire creates a continuity between ceiling and light. It was James's intention to eliminate all elements that would disturb this fluidity. It goes without saying that we didn't want to see the lightsource - but also we didn't want to see any fixtures or fittings at all. Not an easy task considering that the largest part of the luminaire has to be transparent for the light to efficiently pass through. Even the highly advanced technology of the product is not openly displayed but rather only discreetly expressed through the high quality of light.

The common thread in James's work was to design objects with smooth and simple volumes, designing away all visual complexity. With the design of Mellow Light, conceived to be fitted into a grid of ceiling tiles and typically applied in multiples, James extended his concept of unity to the whole ceiling. - Dunja Weber

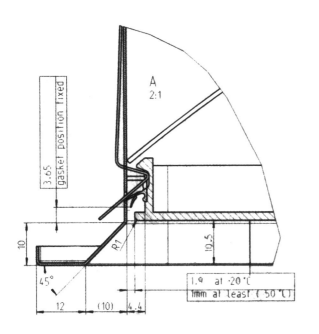

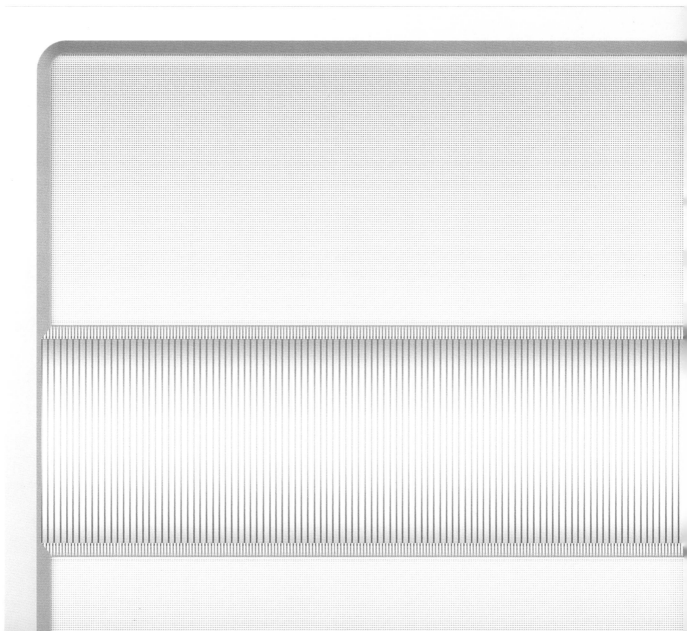

Everybody is surrounded by treasures - by
finds, memories, figures from model railways.
Most get dusty somewhere. I wanted to return
the intrinsic value to these treasures.
Enzo Mari once designed a *wunderkammer* which
I thought was very nice. But I didn't want
to design a system - rather, the focus was
to be on individual 'boxes'. At that time,
fortunately, Christoph Böninger came to visit
me. Six weeks later, he came back with the
first prototypes. The rest: perfect craft
work, bright, untreated ashwood, no screws
but a cover which can be hinged over the
boxes and laterally shifted. - James Irvine

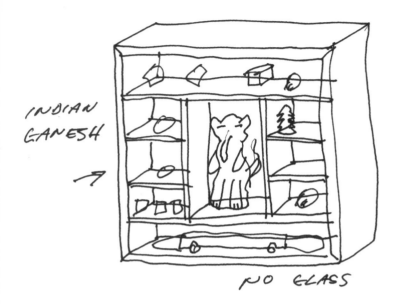

INDIAN
GANESH

NO GLASS

I was invited to take part in an ecodesign competition during the Helsinki Furniture Fair. I realized that when you talk about ecology and design you should not forget quality - if something is durable, it becomes ecological, because you don't have to buy it multiple times. The culture of cheap, throw-away things is really an ecological disaster.

This stool has six large tenon joints, using the fox-tail technique which means that the parts can be wedged together without using glue. I wanted the tenons to express a very strong visible joint. I chose the same wood used to build saunas. And the other thing (which was not part of the brief), is that at the end of the product's life, hopefully after one hundred years, you can even burn it to heat your sauna. - James Irvine

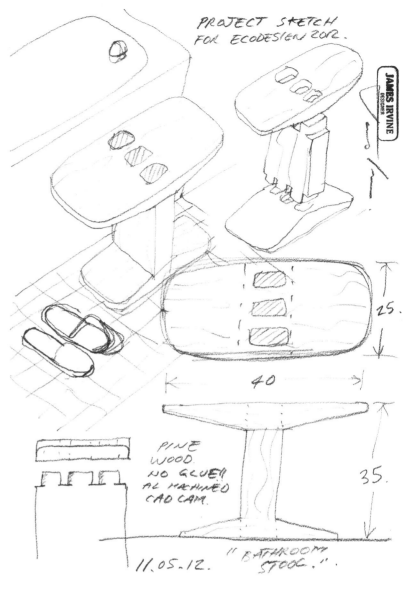

PROJECT SKETCH FOR ECODESIEN 2012.

JAMES IRVINE DESIGNER

25.

40

PINE WOOD. NO GLUE! AL MACHINED CAD CAM.

35.

11.05.12.   " BATHROOM STOOL."

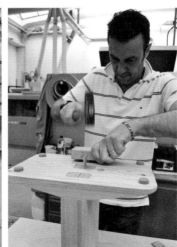

Plastic chairs, which first appeared in the 1960s, are
not a new product typology. However their development
has been a rather Darwinian process. For a few decades
they were stuck using a traditional moulding process.
These were designs with equal wall thicknesses of
the material. Like shells. Hundreds of designs were
developed using the same basic technology. Then at the
turn of the century a revolution happened. Gas-assisted
moulding for one-shot plastic chairs. Forms could be
free with volume. Legs could be thinner like tubes.
Joints could have fluid forms. A series of great chairs
were designed in the early 2000s.

As always, new technologies have a defining
moment when they become available to the designer.
The invention of bentwood by Michael Thonet, the
cantilever tubular steel chair by Mart Stam and the
plywood shell chair so beautifully developed by Jacobsen
and Charles and Ray Eames to name a few. Gas-assisted
moulding is a revolution on a par with these events.

For Arper to embark on the design and production
of a one-shot moulded plastic chair is, in a sense,
a contradiction to the company philosophy. A one-shot
chair seems to dictate a fixed consumer product. More
commodity than flexibility.

Junoesque · adj. (of a woman) tall and shapely. - ORIGIN C19: from the name of Juno,
goddess of ancient Rome and wife of Jupiter, + -ESQUE.

The chair was designed from the beginning as
a product with or without arms. This is already
an unusual characteristic. During development,
it became clear that it would be very
interesting to have a strong differentiation
between the indoor and outdoor versions. This
was solved by having either a closed or an
open back. The open-back version guarantees
that no water is trapped but at the same time
gives a more open and lighter feeling to the
chair. The closed version is more suited to
a dining situation. A modesty back! A more
traditional 'solid' approach. But what really
makes the collection an 'intelligent' Arper
family of products is the possibility of using
upholstered pads on the seat and back. This
lifts the design out of the mire. Above all,
it elevates the image of the one-shot plastic
chair, giving it a new value. More durable,
sophisticated and less casual. Chairs for
the more discerning client at the right price.
- James Irvine

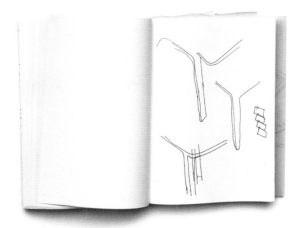

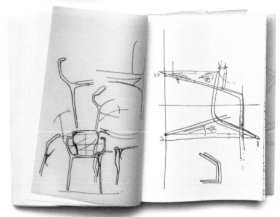

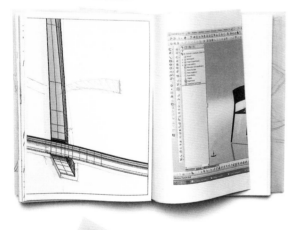

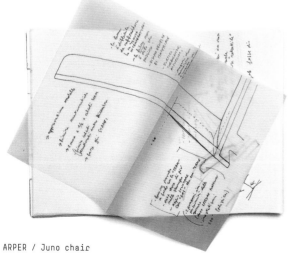

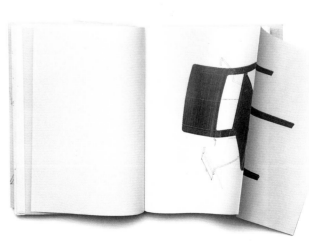

NgispeN is a company that seems to want to enjoy
itself. If I think about furniture to enjoy, I think
about those wonderful time-wasting moments in life.
Those moments when you want to do nothing. Maybe
just spin around and let time drift by. Maybe wait
for someone to come up and say hello. So I thought
of a cone sitting on another cone and where the two
cones meet they rotate. Then I realized it looked
a bit like the nozzle of a rocket engine so I named
the chair Blaster. - James Irvine

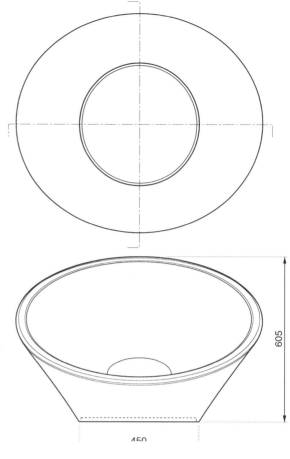

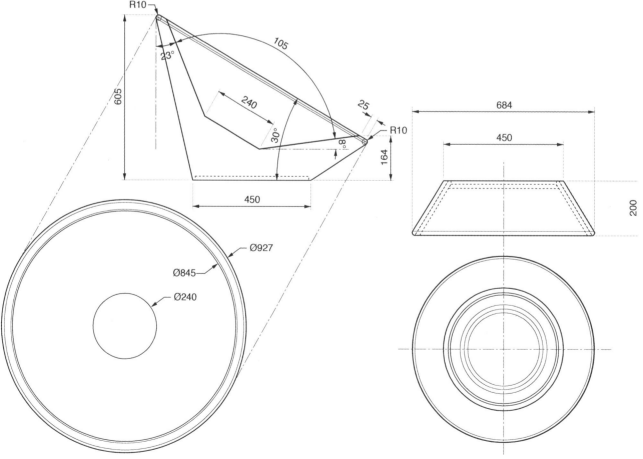

1. SIX

James used to love his visits to Amorim: cork and a good bottle of port - a perfect pairing. I have very pleasant memories of our tours of the 'stripped' trees whilst listening to stories of how cork is processed. How could one not be inspired by a material that is so ancient and so close to humanity? For our project we collected every possible sample of cork: fair or dark, in a variety of grains and shades, and we continued to smell and touch them. We began working on the idea of an architectonic element. Then one day a very happy James showed me a sketch he had done for a bottle-rack. Laughing, he said: 'This idea is the bomb'. As usual, he surprised me and I confess I was puzzled at first. But then the object took shape and Six was born. What better than cork to accommodate, protect, carry and store wine?
- Marialaura Rossiello Irvine

2. STOW IT

Also made from cork, Stow It is a modular element
to be hung on the wall that functions as a
reading-stand and shelf. It also becomes a system,
interconnecting the modules thanks to bottle corks
used as plugs. So here was an architectonic element
which, besides being attractive and functional as
a magazine and bookshelf, also helps to improve the
acoustics of a space. - Marialaura Rossiello Irvine

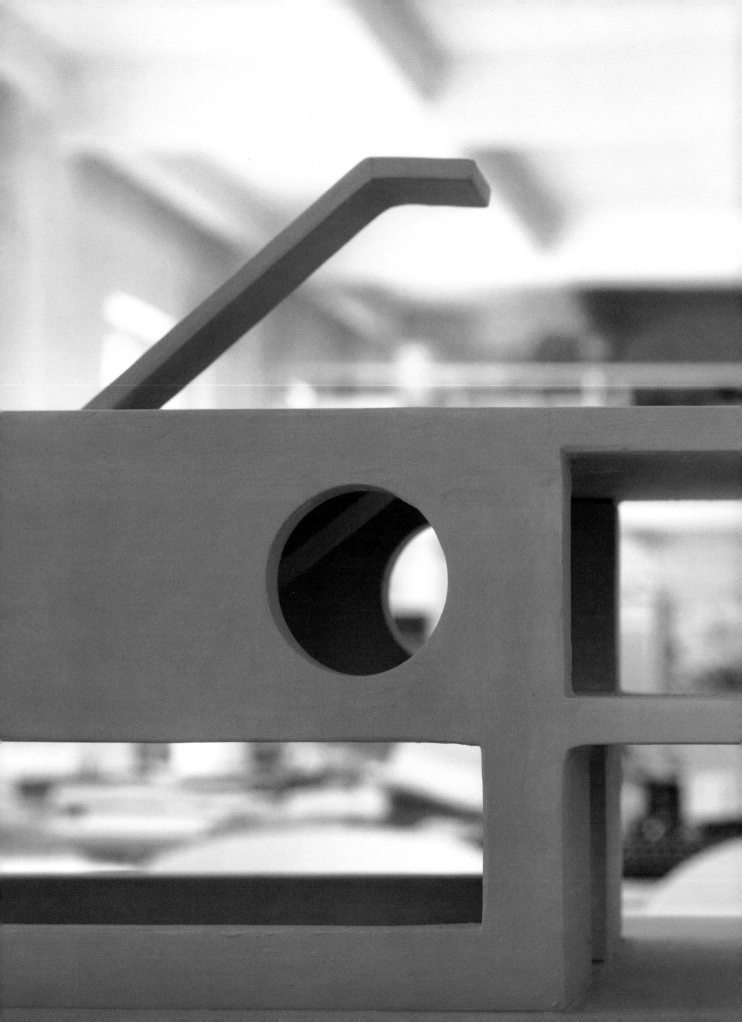

MARIALAURA ROSSIELLO IRVINE

DESIGNING
24/7

Living with James was an amazing adventure and a journey of discovery.

A man of great curiosity and exactitude, he always made me laugh, and a glance from him was enough to give me strength, even at the most difficult moments. I shared ten years with him, during which we built our family – our best project.

April 2001
Experimentation, irony and tales

I first met James at Danese; he was the team's 'young' designer, working with leading figures like Enzo Mari, Paolo Rizzatto and Michele De Lucchi, while I had just joined the team of the new Danese after taking a Masters in Strategic Design at the Polytechnic University of Milan.

For many years Danese was a hothouse of experimentation and research for both of us. James loved working there, he felt free to explore new approaches to forms and technologies. For me it was an endless series of discoveries, and immersing myself in the world of international design was a dream come true. It was like living inside a book about design. I switched from role to role: design development, communication, marketing, production. It was a process of limbering up in order to practise what I had studied: how to combine the culture of design with that of business.

The meetings between James and Carlotta de Bevilacqua, Danese's CEO, were always interesting and enjoyable, with lessons on design and the jokes that were typical of James.

His ideas were fresh and always surprising because they always originated in new viewpoints and different kinds of stimuli: a technical challenge, a personal anecdote, a simple ironic gesture, or a need shared but not expressed. The names and stories of the various designs were always self-explanatory. The Daisy clothes hanger mimics a flower, made of bent metal and in a glaring Day-Glo colour; Superhook is a plastic hook that can 'stay put', hanging from an adhesive strip; Archivio Vivo is a bookstand consisting of a single piece of extruded metal; Hold It is a system of stackable boxes and trays in flexible wood; Make Up is a mirror with a shelf for make-up and Belvedere is a mirror in the form of a map of Italy.

Many designs never reached the production stage, but they were part of a creative process. I remember in particular some of James's designs that didn't get past the prototype stage, like the Bump Box pen-holder that formed a hill in the landscape of the desk; or the EraOra clock, in which discs, instead of hands, went round. I also remember Rismatic, a system of stacking in-trays in extruded metal.

MARIALAURA ROSSIELLO IRVINE

It was during his presentation of Rismatic that I told him rather innocently, 'James, you're pretty good, you know?' He laughed and started to court me; he invited me to dinner at Higuma, his favourite Japanese restaurant. That night we walked across Milan talking non-stop, now and then dropping in at one of our favourite bars. He told me many stories from his past life. James was very good at telling stories.

He talked about the time when, aged four, he hid under a very posh kid's pram in Hyde Park and in a few minutes succeeded in dismantling it, making it fall apart completely, to the huge embarrassment of his mother Betty.

Or, when as a boy in Lanzarote, playing golf with Alan, his father, he struck him right in the front teeth and broke them, then fixed them skilfully using an adhesive containing two components. When they got back from the trip, the dentist himself complimented him on his perfect repair.

Or, when as a young child he gave his first performance on the violin, standing with his back to the audience out of shyness, and when he turned round at the end, he saw they were all red in the face from trying not to giggle. And how, as soon as they burst out laughing, he threw his violin onto the floor and never touched it again.

Or, when in his teens, he was a Boy Scout with the Queen's children in the drawing rooms of Buckingham Palace, and how struck he had been by the toilet paper decorated with the royal crown.

Or, when at Kingston University, he obstinately insisted he wanted to be an artist, and his professor told him nicely to forget about it and be a designer instead.

Or, when during his very first presentation in Italy of a project for Olivetti, in front of the entire management, instead of saying 'from the object descend two columns (*colonne*)', he said 'from the object descend two testicles' (*coglioni*). Even now, the engineers of the old Olivetti remember the Englishman of the two testicles.

Then there was his round-Italy trip as a thirty-year-old, driving the Fiat 600 given to him by Michele De Lucchi.

Prototype for Bump Box for Danese, 2002

And he described how, while working for Toshiba in Tokyo, one Thursday he was late for work because he had a hangover and as an excuse he told his boss he had been to Tokyu Hands department store to do a bit of research. And how his boss, in disbelief, had said 'But Irvine san, Tokyu Hands is closed on Thursdays.'

How, full of excitement, after years of preparation and waiting, he went to his mentor Ettore Sottsass to announce that at long last he had organized a trip to India, where Sottsass had found great inspiration, and Sottsass replied 'Too late, James.'

How he wanted at all costs to learn to draw two circles with both hands at the same time, the way Sottsass could.

How Diego Della Valle, after the presentation of one of his designs for Tod's, gave him a lift in his helicopter but then left him in Parma, from where James had to return to Milan by train, third-class.

Each story was followed by a wink and his characteristic little smile. He made me laugh and laugh. I had fallen in love.

Then one day James turned up at Danese on his BSA motorbike, carrying a small prototype of his Daisy clothes stand, and presented it to me like a flower: we got engaged and a month later we were in India on our first trip together.

Curiosity, exactitude and provocations

James was always curious about everything around him: objects, people, mechanical devices and shapes; even when looking at a pretty woman, his excuse was: '*Cipa*, I'm a designer, I love pleasing shapes!'

He seemed absent-minded when he was talking, but at the same time he took in every detail of our surroundings.

He took masses of photographs, which he then archived. In particular, photos of chairs, chairs and more chairs: a wooden chair with armrests, a wooden chair with one armrest, a wooden chair with no back, a wooden chair with three legs, a metal chair with… James really did design a lot of chairs. Plastic chairs, folding chairs in wood and folding chairs in plastic, wooden chairs, metal chairs with holes, bentwood chairs, chairs in wood and fabric… I've counted them: over fifteen different models actually went into production.

He would often change his mind about a design. He would suddenly turn up with a radically different proposal, saying, 'I realized it didn't really work', and he would come up with a totally new idea. James was capable of turning a design on its head, changing it radically, and filing the previous one away. With no hesitation or regrets, he would pursue his creative impulse, making you feel quite disconcerted. I, on the other hand, would become attached to the initial ideas; I can never abandon them and always try to recover them somehow. He was so precise in his filing that going through the material he archived with that maniacal attention, one can understand perfectly the creative process that lay behind each design. As a matter of fact, for each new project he used to create a 'black book', a folder in which he would gather in chronological order all the 'data' that makes up a design: business cards, the company's brief, initial sketches, emails, correspondence, technical drawings, notes… everything needed to archive a project's history. Once the project had come to an end, the material of the 'black book' was carefully bound, and became a 'white book'. Each design is a free-standing book. In the studio today we have all the projects, going back to 1985, organized in this way.

My ten years with James were a constant process of discovery and a new kind of education for me: I discovered British design, as opposed to my architectural training in the Neapolitan School, which was poetic and a bit airy-fairy. His approach to design was very pragmatic and rigorous, but also full of irony.

I learnt precision, and attention to the smallest detail. My 'approximation', as he liked to call it, used to drive him mad, literally; there was no place for delay, approximation or vagueness.

He loved the fact that I came from Naples, from a culture totally opposite to his own. He had fun mimicking my accent, writing love messages in the Neapolitan dialect, making me listen to an unfamiliar song by Renato Carosone, noticing the figures of Neapolitan women, and wandering around the alleys of Naples looking for objects made following local traditions. That was how some large antlers, small pictures of a glowing Vesuvius, and ceramics with lemons in relief took pride of place in our home.

And so he asked me to marry him. He had planned that moment for months, and there we were on a deserted beach in Mexico one dark night, under the waning moon, he knelt down, took the ring out of his pocket and said, 'Will you do the honour of marrying me?' How could I refuse him? We were in the middle of nowhere, in one of the most dangerous areas in the whole of Mexico…

James and Marialauras' wedding card from Alan Fletcher, 2005

MARIALAURA ROSSIELLO IRVINE

Our discussions about design were endless. James could make you change your mind completely, after first disconcerting you and making you feel angry.

His provocative, challenging comments revealed a different starting point from which to approach a project. It was invaluably enriching; he always had a clear view of things and then, suddenly, a flash of intuition. Putting himself face to face with someone else was crucial: his 'provocations' would usually lead to long discussions, lasting well into the night. A short pause would be enough for us to digest his reasoning in silence, and then the discussion would resume. He was almost always right.

I remember in particular a project in marble, commissioned in 2012 by a Turkish company, IMIB. James developed an initial idea for a carport with a staircase giving access to a roof garden but he wasn't convinced. One morning he woke up, changed his mind and designed a table, suspended under a pergola held up by four ropes, which he named Suspense. For me his ideas were almost always valid because each new proposal, though designed to fulfil a specific purpose, expressed an approach that was pragmatic, and met the requirements of actual production.

For Amorim, the leading Portuguese cork producer, James also started off with a very precise idea, but ended up with a completely different one: the initial idea of a sound-absorbing lamp became a shelf designed to be hung on a wall, creating a system in which corks were used to fit the parts together. It is an architectural concept, which, besides being pleasing to the eye and practical for holding books and magazines, also helps to improve the acoustics of the space. The design is called Stow It.

James's intuitions were way ahead of my constant analysis. He intuited. Full stop.

I remember the project for a bench in Milan (I forget the precise date). James, the only 'foreigner', was at last able to design for his adopted city. After twenty-five years he finally felt he was a Milanese!

James developed an idea that at first sight could have met with criticism, but as soon as you realized what material was used – Ta-da! Ecology! He used

Panchina per Milano bench for Coro, 2005

a type of recycled plastic that unfortunately looked like fake marble. When he learned of the fierce online opposition to his bench he was mortified, but he took heart when he heard that the mayor of Busto Arsizio had ordered four of the benches for the town square.

James's vision of the world was made up of so many utopias, his extreme correctness brought him into constant conflict with a country like Italy, with its myriad contradictions. It drove him mad, but then he'd go to one of his favourite restaurants that served traditional Milanese fare, and would come to terms with it all.

In Italy James could realize his dream and his vision of design: to be able to experiment with craftsmen from the Brianza, to work in direct contact with the most diverse aspects of a business, to be able to design anything from a bus to a pen, to travel the world but always with the strength and the awareness of being a pig-headed Brit in the Bel Paese.

But motorbikes were his greatest passion: for him, riding a motorbike was freedom, getting covered in oil his great delight, taking it apart and putting it together his everlasting dream. He would spend hours studying engines and speeds, watching videos on the classic British bikes – BSA, Triton, Triumph, Norton – reading books on the American Lockheed SR-71 Blackbird reconnaissance plane, and watching YouTube clips on the construction of early twentieth-century British locomotives.

And then our children, Giacomo and Giorgio, came along. His dream had come true: to 'build a family'.

James couldn't wait to design for his boys: the wooden child's face for Muji, the petrol tanker for TuBeUs, the floor cushions Bruchi for Play+. And lots of other projects that are still in a drawer, never completed.

Of all the objects James designed, our children love the Blaster chair best, one of the last projects he carried out for NgispeN, in 2012. Richard Hutten, NgispeN's art director, had asked him to be part of the team. After many experiments and changes of direction, the design came to life: a revolving armchair that is James through and through: two cones that meet and rotate. The kids use it as a spinning top to launch themselves into space.

James loved to surprise. He could have unexpected exchanges with unexpected people: a gift-wrapped parcel containing an object specially designed for you, a phone call asking you to join a project, an invitation to your favourite restaurant, an email containing a joke, at the very moment you needed it. To surprise and involve. Even now I get these unexpected surprises, and I love the thought that they are 'from an unknown British hero'.

One day James was contacted by Marsotto, a leading Italian company specializing in marble: they wanted him to be their art director. He had no hesitation in accepting a new challenge and in building a new team with a shared vision of design: Jasper, Konstantin, Naoto, Thomas, Alberto, Maddalena and Ross.

James put so much passion into developing Marsotto Edizioni in collaboration with its entrepreneurial owners, Costanza and Mario Marsotto. It was almost as though he felt the company was to some extent his own, and he felt keenly his responsibility as art director. The intuition that led him from the start was to make marble 'light', suitable for use in everyday objects: tables, occasional tables, seats, console tables. James had a very clear vision of what he needed to do, both in writing briefs and in establishing the means of communication within a company, from organizing photo shoots explaining the design to setting up exhibitions.

James simply loved to 'orchestrate'. He was capable of synthesis, good judgement and great modesty.

Wooden petrol tanker for ToBeUs, 2012

James always wanted the Studio Irvine team to be small and feared losing control of the project. He was maniacal and very controlling. Nothing was left to chance, down to the smallest detail.

His planning was such that we almost always closed the studio at six in the evening, only to continue over an aperitif, talking and discussing. It was often at those times that ideas emerged.

Dinner with friends, too, was always a great time for sharing and argument, with everyone defending his or her own point of view. At the homes of Stefano and Elisa Giovannoni, of George Sowden and Nathalie Du Pasquier, Joel and Kaijsa Berg, we would spend endless hours discussing politics, design and new business ideas, telling jokes and invariably talking about food. Those are unforgettable moments for me, full of richness and passion.

For James, the right choice of restaurant was a sacred matter. He had a long list of names, telephone numbers, proprietors and favourite waiters, and obviously of the right dishes to order. Organization was his forte.

He had a passion for food of every culture, its preparation, presentation and colours. Nothing was left to chance, even at home, everything had to have its own rules and logic. For example, at every meal the vegetables had to be of different colours, never the same. The ideal combination was carrots, potatoes and Brussels sprouts – orange, yellow and green. Everything cooked to perfection and piping hot.

And then we found out that James was ill.

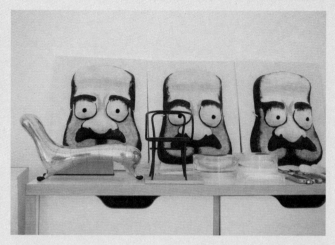

The production process for the papier mache Daruma mask, 2012

May 2011
A love of life, making things by hand and
collecting traditional objects

James loved life, always pursued new challenges, never gave up. Every time he designed a new object he saw himself as its first purchaser.

His passion for objects grew with time: on most days a 'surprise parcel' would be delivered to the house or the studio. Almost daily James would order online things that he needed for research into new objects or as small gifts, but also many things that reminded him of his deep British roots. They included Victorian Staffordshire figurines, traditional English ceramic objects made in the nineteenth century to decorate the mantelpieces of working-class homes. I used to dismiss them as kitsch, but he would say, 'Look at the details'. That's how I began to look at the details of every object: its shape, its colours, its imperfections.

Over time I got to know all the characters who inhabited our home: the man with the sheep, the young girl sitting on a goat, the harvester with her sheaf of wheat, Saint George and the Dragon, a family group with sheep, the 'fairing' that's a pen-holder in the form of a sultan, the Scottish Highlanders with their goat, the hunter with his dog and gun, the royal children, the married couple and the spaniels.

The collections were part of a journey through design and the discovery of the tradition that lies behind each object. After the figures came the lids of early twentieth-century British ceramic pots for a whole variety of things: Burgess's Anchovy Paste and Home-Made Potted Meats from London, William Darling

Tooth Paste and Oriental Tooth Paste from Manchester, Patum Peperium from Essex, Fortnum & Mason's Caviar, Cherry Tooth Paste, Cold Cream, and so on.

This period was closely followed by James's enthusiasm for Japanese vintage paper masks, and one day he asked me to make a papier mache mask. None of us had the faintest idea how to do it. James had been invited to participate in a group exhibition devoted to Ito Jakuchu, an eighteenth-century Japanese artist. Each designer was asked to create a piece inspired by his work.

James fell in love with a drawing of the Giant Daruma by Ito Jakuchu, so he wanted to make the drawing three-dimensional by making a mask of the Giant Daruma, according to Japanese tradition. A challenge to our craftsmanship and manual dexterity. We made the mould and the plaster cast, and then we applied layers of various kinds of paper, using a special glue. Once the glued layers had dried, we proceeded to the painting stage. In the end we made three masks. I never thought we'd manage it, nor did James.

James had a particular liking for the salt cellars found in restaurants, and he used to study them obsessively. However, since for him perfection in salt was only to be found in Maldon sea salt, crumbled between one's fingers, the ideal salt cellar had to be a simple little bowl. Of course we also went through the phase of regularly buying salt cellars on eBay: currently our studio boasts a collection of about a hundred.

He also continued to buy Märklin train sets, complete with level crossing, station, little figures and mountains. He loved to assemble them on the conference table when the children came to the studio. The three of them would spend hours imitating the puffing of the steam train.

James was obsessed with postcards; he always bought three the same, and loved sending them instead of a formal letter. He used to keep one for his collection. I have thousands of postcards at home, from all over the world.

In 2012 the same 'journey' and James's love for crafts led him to design a set of dominoes in connection with a special project organized by *Wallpaper** magazine. In this case, however, he decided to use an art form typical of my birthplace: the cameo.

For this, too, we tried to emulate the centuries-old technique for carving shells and make a cameo of James's BSA motorbike, to be set into a domino made of Corian, all this to be skilfully handled by an historic Neapolitan firm, the De Simone Fratelli.

In 2013 Alessandro Mendini invited James to participate in the first Milano Makers, an exhibition devoted to designer-makers based in Milan. Its theme was terracotta. James had the idea of defying conventions regarding size, and sketched a piece of architecture – his architecture – and called it 'I wish I was an Architect'. It was his dream house. I had it made and now it has pride of place in the lobby of our studio.

James's method was to analyse, sketch, start to translate the drawing into a file, sketch, simplify, discuss, correct, print, build a maquette in our workshop, examine it, live with it for a while, discuss, sketch, cut, smooth down, update the three-dimensional drawing, digest, correct, reach agreement all round, bind, and send off.

When he was in his studio among his things, he was happy, we were happy.

James did a lot of drawing and sketching and filed every idea that occurred to him. He sketched with such precision, with shading and everything. His favourite tools were his Pilot 0.3 pencil, his Uni-ball Vision Elite pen, his Cangini Filippi diary, his sketching paper – simple, pristine A4 sheets.

Each 1 January James gave us all a Cangini Filippi diary and made us enter all our appointments with a Pilot 0.3 pencil. A pencil, never a pen! So that we could rub things out and not be 'imprecise', a word he loved. Of course, not only did I use a pen, but I used that diary only for the first few months of the year. It infuriated him.

For James, the last word in shoes was Florsheim slip-ons. He used to buy three pairs of them a year. Now I have exactly thirty pairs. As for bags, it was strictly Valextra; for jeans, Levi's, for belts Paul Smith, and then Aspesi shirts, a Crombie coat and an Aviakit leather jacket.

His vision of design and of life was rigorous, generous and ironic.

James taught me to aim for simplification.

James taught me to look at what's around me, and study the details.

James taught me about synthesis and a humble approach to design.

James taught me not to question myself too much, but simply to do.

James taught us to enjoy life. Enjoy life.

And then James flew away.

18 February 2013, at 0.00 hours. Punctual as ever.

I am happy to have lived with James, and today I have beside me his creative legacy, his outlook on life and the practice of design, which have enriched our journey; I have never had doubts about it; Studio Irvine lives on.

MARIALAURA ROSSIELLO IRVINE